Routledge Reviv

The Apple

First published in 1951, this book is based on a course of lectures on poetry and prose given at Cambridge University during the long vacations of 1946-1950. A request for lectures of this kind came originally from a group of science students and the response was such that a course of this nature ran yearly. The purpose was to provide students from disciplines other than the humanities with the opportunity to feed their interest in English poetry and literature.

The Apple and the Spectroscope

being lectures on poetry designed (in the main)
for science students

T. R. Henn

Routledge
Taylor & Francis Group

First published in 1951
by Methuen & Co. Ltd

This edition first published in 2013 by Routledge
2 Park Square, Milton Park, Abingdon, Oxon, OX14 4RN

Simultaneously published in the USA and Canada
by Routledge
711 Third Avenue, New York, NY 10017

Routledge is an imprint of the Taylor & Francis Group, an informa business

The publisher would like to thank The Royal Literary Fund for their kind
permission to quote "A Map of Verona" by Henry Reed

Publisher's Note
The publisher has gone to great lengths to ensure the quality of this reprint but
points out that some imperfections in the original copies may be apparent.

Disclaimer
The publisher has made every effort to trace copyright holders and welcomes
correspondence from those they have been unable to contact.

A Library of Congress record exists under ISBN: 52026026

ISBN 13: 978-0-415-83436-0 (hbk)
ISBN 13: 978-0-203-49739-5 (ebk)
ISBN 13: 978-0-415-83438-4 (pbk)

THE APPLE AND
THE SPECTROSCOPE

being
Lectures on Poetry designed (in the main) for Science Students

by

T. R. HENN

C.B.E., M.A., Hon. Litt.D. (Dublin) Hon. L.L.D. (Victoria)

with a Foreword by

PROFESSOR SIR LAWRENCE BRAGG
F.R.S., O.B.E., M.C., D.SC.

METHUEN & CO. LTD., LONDON
11 New Fetter Lane, E.C.4

First published in 1951

School edition 1962
Second edition 1965

CATALOGUE NO. 2/7545/6

REPRINTED BY LITHOGRAPHY IN GREAT BRITAIN
BY JARROLD AND SONS LTD, NORWICH

And pluck till time and times are done
The silver apples of the moon,
The golden apples of the sun.

W. B. YEATS

But you, dear boy, with your twenty-five impartial years,
Can perform the judgement of Paris,
Can savour, consider, and award the apple
With a cool hand. You will find an apple
Over there by the spectroscope.

CHRISTOPHER FRY

For every one pupil who needs to be guarded from a weak excess of sensibility there are three who need to be awakened from the slumbers of cold vulgarity. The task of the modern educator is not to cut down jungles but to irrigate forests. By starving the sensibility of our pupils we only make them easier prey to the propagandist when he comes.

C. S. LEWIS

FOREWORD

I WELCOME the invitation to write an introduction to this series of lectures, because it affords me an opportunity to express our gratitude as scientists to our arts colleagues in the university who have given their time and thought to preparing a special course for science undergraduates, and so made possible this extremely interesting experiment. The numbers which have crowded the lecture-room and the deep interest taken in the lectures have been convincing proof that a very real need is being met.

Anxiety is often expressed about early specialization and the narrowness of outlook which it engenders, especially in the case of our science students. The rising standards of scholarship and university entrance examinations are commonly blamed for the pressure put upon the schools, but I believe this to be merely a symptom and in seeking for a cure we must look deeper for the cause. The competition for places in the universities and for financial aid is forcing the pace, and both university and school teachers are being swept along by a machine they have not yet learnt to control. I think it is generally true that the former desire a wider course at school as ardently as the latter, and are often embarrassed by the plethora of specialized knowledge of university entrants, which can so easily be superficial if it is not based on a good background of general culture. No one party or the other can be singled out for blame for narrowness and specialization. It is an unfortunate result of a good movement, the throwing open of the universities to able young people in the whole country. Universities and schools must combine to find the best answer to the problem.

But when the students enter the universities, we have the

planning of their courses entirely in our own hands, and set our own standards. If they do not get from the university the broad outlook and sympathy with all forms of intellectual adventure which it should give them, the fault is ours alone. Many of us have felt uneasily that we are not taking the responsibility with sufficient seriousness.

As the author of these lectures says in his preface, the success of these Long Vacation courses has encouraged one of the scientific faculties to plan similar courses throughout the academic year. One lecture a week may seem a very small part of the time-table to devote to so important an educational project, but I believe that the result will be quite disproportionately great. Such lectures enable the students to meet and hear the universities' leaders on the arts side, men who would otherwise be merely names to them. Even if few in number, they open vistas and arouse interest. The science student gets a sense of values and aesthetic appreciation of great achievements in fields other than his own, and his life is enriched by a deeper understanding of literature. I feel sure, too, that the object we have in view is better attained by courses of the kind where attendance is voluntary, than it would be by any formal curriculum and subsequent examination.

Quite apart from the broadening of outlook, there is another reason why the study of literature is of essential importance to the scientist. Some scientists may have been content to seek knowledge for their own mental satisfaction alone, with complete indifference to imparting their experience to others ; they correspond to the ascetic. But they are rare, and the normal scientist finds the deepest pleasure in exchanging his thoughts with his fellow men. Science is becoming so vast and specialized that it is increasingly difficult to keep abreast of development. Just as gold is mined from the earth with infinite labour to be buried again in the earth in vaults, so new knowledge may only too easily be buried in scientific journals until with the lapse of time it can no longer be of interest or influence the progress of science. It is as important to present new knowledge in a form in which it can be assimilated and its essential import realized as it is to discover it, and this presentation is an art akin to poetry and literature. As Mr. Henn says in one of his lectures, the potential must be raised until the spark can pass from one mind to another. Many of the great leaders of science knew this well, and their papers are a delight to read because by happy analogy or clever turn of phrase they give one that glorious feeling of becoming stronger oneself, of being able to comprehend something easily which had previously seemed infinitely complex, because the master has taught us what is " good style " in thought. The real joy of science lies not in accumulating new facts, but in seeing new relations and developing new and more masterly ways of thinking about them. The close connection between science on the one hand, and philosophy and literature on the other, may have been partly lost sight of during the recent age of scientific exploration, but it is inevitably emerging again and it is the duty of our universities to assign to it its full importance. These interesting and stimulating lectures were deeply appreciated when they were delivered, and I am glad that they are now to be published.

W. L. BRAGG

PREFACE

I

IN the spring of 1947 a group of science students at Cambridge approached the university with a request that lectures should be organized, for their special needs, on some aspect of English Literature ; these to be given in the Long Vacation Term, when the science courses were less exacting as regards the time that they demanded. It was not very clear just what it was they required : but the General Board of the Faculties authorized the course as an experiment, and a small committee representing the students and the Faculty Board of English discussed a possible syllabus. The Heads of Scientific Departments and the Faculty Lecturers supported the course, and arranged time-tables so as to allow men to attend.

The first lectures were given in July and August 1947 ; and were repeated, in varying forms but with the same general plan, in subsequent years. The response to them, as evidenced by a crowded lecture-theatre and an obvious interest in following up the problems raised by the lectures, was a little overwhelming. It was apparent that these lectures satisfied some need, not easily to be formulated, for a number of the students.

Many of the audience, who came afterwards to informal discussions, were obviously sensitive to poetry, and had read widely. A somewhat larger group suggested that literature had been spoilt for them by inefficient or uninspired teaching at school : the kind of teaching often thought good enough for the ' English subsidiary ' subject that is frequently the scientist schoolboy's only opportunity for this kind of enlargement of his horizon. Two Shakespeare plays with their contexts and ' stock ' questions, or half a dozen pseudo-classics chosen (to some extent at least) for their ' examinable ' qualities, had failed to convince them that it was worth while going on. This group came, I think, because it was prepared to be interested in literature, and to make a fresh start, from new assumptions and with new objectives. A third group, undetermined as to numbers because disinclined to speak of their problems, appeared to be seeking for elements in literature that were to be complementary to their scientific work; some ordering or stabilizing of their growing thoughts.

The criticism of selected pieces of verse and prose raised an immediate difficulty in the provision of some text which the members of the audience could have before them ; and a booklet was therefore printed and issued for each group of lectures. The poems and passages had to be reasonably short, and an attempt was made to select those which lent themselves to a consideration of the kinds of values which could be readily related, in lectures, to ' the art of living '. Further, they had to be chosen so as to afford instances of widely different techniques and periods. In practice, it became apparent that some examples ' worked ' in this context, and others did not ; and therefore the booklet was revised each year.

An audience of this kind and size includes a wide range of levels, background and knowledge, and the technique of lecturing had therefore to be somewhat different from the normal academic approach. The object was not primarily to impart information, but to stimulate a desire to acquire it. The treatment was therefore an ' expanding ' one, and interjections, parallels, and ' collateral considerations ' seemed to be justified as serving that end. No initial bibliography was given ; instead, the lecturer was ' At Home ' at stated hours to those who wished for advice on their reading. And because those who attended were, in the main, scientists, it seemed appropriate to make some use of the visual and intellectual appeal of diagrams and formulæ, though with full warning as to their limitations and inaccuracies.

The discussions with members of the audience, and with others who had read the notes, suggested that there was some demand for an introduction of this kind for those who had had little opportunity of serious reading. It seemed possible also that this particular audience might be typical of others at a similar stage of exploration. The lectures have therefore been written out as nearly as possible in the manner in which they were delivered, with a typical ' booklet ' printed as Appendix I. The passage from T. S. Eliot's *Waste Land* proved one of the most successful extracts : not only because of the wide appeal of the poem, but because of the allusive technique that lent itself to quasi-mathematical explanation. Two passages from Shakespeare, included in a previous year, have been added ; for it was obvious that Shakespeare offered the best prospect of bringing literature back to the scientist ; though the manner of doing it in a single lecture is a fantastic problem, with no solution except through the possible provision of an initial stimulus. A lecture on two passages from the Bible, not originally included in this series, has been added in response to various suggestions : since the Bible appears to have suffered even more than Shakespeare from forced and misdirected consideration, in schools, and from the deadening effect of unapprehended repetition in compulsory chapel services. There is, in addition, what one can only describe as a *fear* of reading the Bible, because of the aura that has been built about it, and because such a mystical attitude towards its contents tends to inhibit any enjoyment or appreciation of its qualities. And, much as I admire C. S. Lewis' brilliance of argument, I cannot subscribe to his proposition that it "excludes or repels the merely aesthetic approach ".[1] Those who are brought to re-read it for its merits as literature may possibly come in time to read it as a ' sacred book '.

[1] C. S. Lewis, *The Literary Impact of the Authorized Version* (1950)

One result of these experimental lectures was the decision of the Department of Physics to organize regular courses for its men during the Michaelmas and Easter Terms. One course was on Classical Philosophy and the Ancient World, the other on English Literature. To do that, the Department deliberately sacrificed part of its time-table. Among the lectures requested for the English Course were two on the outlines of English literature. The task of providing an introduction on such a tiny scale presented obvious difficulties. It seemed best to provide the audience with a printed pamphlet of selected authors, works, and contemporary events to fix them in some sort of relationship in time. In conjunction with such a pamphlet, and some advice as to its use, the attempt was made to give an overall picture, which was necessarily a personal one and in broad outline, of the main movements of thought in their relation to literature. And, because such an outline presupposed some initial stimulus such as might have arisen from the lectures that had been given previously, it seemed appropriate to reverse the logical order and to place these 'Notes for an Introduction to English Literary History' at the end instead of at the beginning of this book.

On the other side of the picture, the University is organizing a series of lectures, somewhat on the lines of the Royal Institution Lectures, for arts men : and this is perhaps a greater need than that of the scientist for literature. For the latter has always sufficient background to understand the language that his fellow-student is using : and if his own background, at home or at school, has been a favourable one, he will often have a very fair idea of the outlook of the men reading arts. But the converse is not true : the scientist's whole manner of thinking, and still more his technical vocabulary, will often be quite outside the field of the arts student. Under favourable conditions of college life there will be a good deal of mutual discussion, of intercourse through literary societies and so forth, that may help to bridge the gap ; but this, though of immense potential value, is by its nature haphazard in operation. And too often the pressure of work in science subjects, the long hours in laboratories, leave no time for those hours of discussion, in twos and threes, which are, after all, the periods when so much of the real growth of a university goes on.

It is often said that the remedy for all this compartmented life lies in the home background, or in a broader curriculum in schools. As to the first, it seems to me that every condition of modern life—its haste, the wireless, television and cinema, the general complexity of living—is steadily making this kind of home more rare. It is surprising how few undergraduates of to-day can rely on a room of their own during the vacation; when essential reading must be done. As for the schools, they are the victims (and will probably continue to be so) of the enormous pressure from the universities—themselves overwhelmed with applicants—whose scholarship standards have steadily grown more specialized and more narrow. The scholarship papers for a schoolboy of eighteen do not compare badly, in science subjects, with the degree papers of twenty years ago. The schools are forced to specialize, to pack their time-tables in the advanced subjects, and to give the minimum of attention to the ' subsidiaries '. Nor are the so-called ' General Papers ' which complement the special subjects of much value in encouraging a wider outlook ; their operation is too often uncertain, and their scope and composition observe few fixed principles.

4

It is possible that a remedy may one day be found in the form of a *concordat* between universities and schools : the one sacrificing something of its standards to encourage a wider outlook, the other taking the complementary subjects more seriously. And here there is a suggestion which may be of value. Too often the senior science forms in a school are given their smattering of ' English ' by the English staff ; sprayed by them with a dilute culture, one eye on the examination results. Such a form is apt to regard the arts master with suspicion. Is it impracticable to suggest that one remedy might be to organize special courses in English for the senior science masters themselves, and let them teach their own forms in their own language ?

At Harvard, I. A. Richards, one of the four university—not faculty—professors, has been working on his project of bringing undergraduates back to the roots of human thought : to put before them again the basis on which our civilization is largely built. Among those roots are the Bible, Plato, Homer ; Shakespeare, Montaigne ; with some of the later philosophers. It is too early to judge what effect this teaching may have on the minds of those who will one day be the leaders of the people. But there seems to be no shadow of doubt, on every side, that some such enlightenment must take place if the scientist is to learn to live outside the rising walls of the laboratory. But it is not the scientist only : it is indeed all those . . . "in places where the spring-time of the local life has been forgotten, and the harvest is a memory only, and the straw has been turned into bricks."[1]

[1] J. M. Synge, Preface to *The Playboy of the Western World*.

ACKNOWLEDGEMENTS

MY thanks for permission to quote are due the following—

Mr. Christopher Fry and The Oxford University Press for the title and the quotation from *Venus Observed* :

Mr. T. S. Eliot and Messrs. Faber & Faber for part of *The Fire Sermon* :

Mrs. Yeats and Messrs. Macmillan for W. B. Yeats' *Consolation, Stream and Sun at Glendalough, The Stare's Nest by my Window,* and *Before the World was Made* from *Collected Poems* ; and *Lapis Lazuli* from *Last Poems and Plays.*

Messrs. Macmillan for Thomas Hardy's *Ah, are you digging on my grave ?* from *Collected Poems.*

Mr. Walter de la Mare and Messrs. Constable for *The Scribe* :

Mr. Roy Campbell and Messrs. Boriswood for a passage from *The Georgiad* :

Mr. Henry Reed and Messrs Jonathan Cape for *Naming of Parts* (from *A Map of Verona*) :

Mr. F. L. Lucas and Messrs. Chatto & Windus for the quotation from *Authors Dead and Living.*

I am also indebted to the British Broadcasting Corporation for permission to use part of the lecture on Marvell's *To His Coy Mistress,* which was broadcast, though in a different form, in the series *The Making of a Poem* ; to Messrs. A. & C. Cooper for the photographs of Blake's *Pity* and Crome's *Thistle and Water Vole* ; to the Trustees of the National Gallery for Holbein's *The Ambassadors* ; and to the Trustees of The British Museum for Blake's *The Sick Rose.*

I am grateful to many friends for their help ; and in particular to Professor Basil Willey, Dr. R. T. H. Redpath, W. G. Ingram, and Peter Allt for their advice and assistance with the proofs ; and to my friends and pupils whose views are incorporated in the list of books in the appendix. And if, in the long process of shaping materials which I have used, I have omitted to make acknowledgement of my debt to others, I hope the omissions may be forgiven.

CONTENTS

ILLUSTRATIONS

MAPS

Some Considerations on the Methods of Poetry

MY object in these lectures is to offer some suggestions regarding the mechanisms and technique of poetry. I shall illustrate them by certain arbitrarily chosen examples, which (in view of the difficulty of bringing in books) I have had printed for you. We shall consider two or three of these poems at each lecture. I do not think you should take notes ; at the end of the little booklet is a blank half-sheet for possible definitions, and you can if you like scribble rough notes in the margins of the poems themselves.

These poems are chosen to suggest to you, as far as possible, the application of poetry to life ; that is, they each deal with one or more attitudes to life, which I shall try to analyse as we come to them. And for the moment I am taking Dr. Johnson's phrase : " What should books teach but the art of living ? " as a kind of reference point. We shall try to see later what that phrase may mean to-day : and afterwards, perhaps, what Matthew Arnold meant by his phrase : " Poetry is a criticism of life."

To start with, then, we can consider the components of a poem. These are, very roughly, *Diction* and *Rhythm*. Words are set in a certain pattern or organization. These patterns will have normally a recurrent quality : hence *versus* (returning) for verse, just as *prosus* (straight on) for prose. To denote this pattern we shall use the symbol P.

Rhythm is usually organised as metre, ' sections of rhythm '. It comprises stress, tone, and pitch. It is, for our purposes, a quality which produces the *impression* of a proportion between the events, or groups of events of which a sound sequence is composed.[1] Note the word 'impression'; we tend to hear rhythm in any repeating sequence, such as the beat of wheels in a train, without necessarily demanding an exact mathematical relationship between its components.

We know comparatively little about the psycho-physiological effects of rhythm. Changes that occur in response to it may include a variation in the pulse-rate, and even a change in the chemical composition of the blood. For our purposes, however, we can regard it as having some or all of the following effects upon us :

(a) a stimulus to increased awareness and receptivity.
(b) the imposition of a pattern upon a complex fusion of thought and emotion.
(c) a kind of 'charging' of words with a greater potential of meaning or meanings.

Diction we can consider under two headings :

(a) the organization of words into this rhythmical pattern, *P*.
(b) the use of words for the purpose of imagery : that is the establishment of relationships between two objects or ideas, and the consequent suggestion of their related values.

This last is such an important aspect of poetry that we must consider it in some detail. We can deal with it first under two simple headings, Simile and Metaphor : the first a comparison introduced by *like* or *as*, the second a direct identification.

Now consider what occurs in our normal methods of using imagery. When Burns says " My love is like a red red rose," the image is so hackneyed that we tend to forget what the first poet who made that comparison may have had in mind. The duplicated *red* merely means that the rose is intensely, or perhaps,

---

[1] E. A. Sonnenschein, *Rhythm.*

' valuably ', red. If we look at the problem in terms of a valve, we have the girl and the rose represented by anode and cathode respectively. What in fact has happened is that certain particles of meaning have streamed across from the rose and attached themselves to the girl. Some of these are: colour, texture, perfection of a short-lived maturity, and the passionate colour

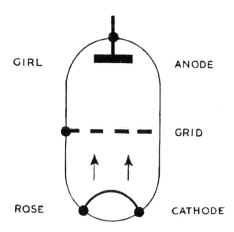

red—for blood, royalty, dignity. But it is apparent that there is also a kind of screen or suppressor in the intervening space, a screen that lets certain kinds of particles pass through, and stops others : and this screening function will depend on the context of the poem, and on the conventions of the poet and his age. When Herrick says

> Gather ye rosebuds while ye may

he is exploiting one kind of significance only : the thought of the rosebud opening as virginity passes to womanhood. When George Herbert writes of it :

> Sweet rose, whose hue angrie and brave
> Bids the rash gazer wipe his eye :
> Thy root is ever in its grave,
>   And thou must die.

—he is bringing together the two thoughts of admiration and death. When the Elizabethan poet speaks perpetually of the eating canker at the heart of the rose as a symbol of corrupted or corruptible womanhood, he is doing something different from, and much less complicated than, the thing that Blake is trying to express in the little poem on your sheet, *The Sick Rose*.

As a further example of the 'conventional' screening, consider the simple simile *The man was as brave as a lion*. It is clear that we have allowed to pass over from lion to man certain conventional attributes of the heraldic lion : the king of beasts, courage, ferocity, and so forth. We have shut off by our screen the lion's cowardliness, his mange, his parasites. The same sort of process goes on continually ; but many of the images in common use we accept so superficially and rapidly that we scarcely think of their implications, of their history, or of the significance they had when the image was first struck out.

Now if we use another electrical figure for the working of a metaphor, that of a spark jumping a gap (and providing a sudden illumination), the width of the gap will vary with different images. Our man-lion comparison involved a smaller gap than the girl-rose. But the gap may be of any width: provided only that a spark can be forced across it. So when Edith Sitwell writes :

> The light is braying like an ass

she is attempting to produce an impression of a stridency, or harshness, in the quality of the light. When Eliot writes :

> I am aware of the damp souls of housemaids
> Sprouting despondently at area gates

the same process is at work ; the gap is wider, the voltage of the imagination required to bridge the gap is greater.

Now the electrical simile for this sparking across the gap can be taken a stage further. The 'normal' voltage of our imagination is always, to some extent, present ; the gap is bridged with ease, provided it is narrow, or has been narrowed by convention or usage ; but if it is wide, or unusual, a greater voltage must be produced, by some means or other, if the reader is to receive the image. That voltage may be thought of as generated in some or all of the following ways :

(a) By the excitement produced in, and by, the poem itself. (We have noted already the stimulus effect of rhythm.)
(b) By the poet's *usage* : that is, by the manner in which he accustoms us to his way of thinking in relation to images.
(c) By the historical *tradition* in which he is working, and which we can understand by a study of his time.

We shall see later on examples of all these ways of bridging the spark gap, of making the images acceptable.

So far we have dealt with ' simple ' images, simile or metaphor. We can carry them a stage further. In making comparisons of this kind, we are really attempting

(a) to synthesize certain aspects of two disparates to form a third, and/or
(b) to draw together the resources of different kinds of meaning to form a third kind of meaning, *which is expressible in no other way*.

We shall consider examples at a later stage.

For this is the final justification of all poetry : that it seeks to express a peculiar fusion of ideas and emotions which are normally on the edge of consciousness, or even beyond it. We have seen that its rhythmic structure produces an increased awareness, an excitement both emotional and intellectual. By means of imagery it is expressing a particular kind of synthesis of meaning, perhaps best suggested in terms of a moving point, 'T', perceived in a three-dimensional field (one dimension being the emotional stimulus or ' potential ' excited by the form), and related to two

5

reference points, ' O ' and ' I ', which may be regarded (for the purposes of this illustration) as being stable. The third dimension would be represented by certain *subjective* values given to both object and image by the reader himself.

Now with this in mind, we can distinguish several kinds of imagery with which we shall be concerned. There is first what we may call traditional imagery ; which we often accept carelessly, because we are so accustomed to it. Its roots may be in the Bible, or Homer, or Plato, or Shakespeare. There are instances by the hundred: the hart desiring the water brooks, the valley of the shadow of death,[1] the slings and arrows of outrageous fortune, the group of images that compare the spirit to a bird ; and so on. Of them I would only suggest at this stage that all of them are well worth looking into, to see what lies beneath that easily-accepted surface.

Then there is the matter of personal imagery ; the peculiar choice that a poet may exercise because of his own experience, his special reading, and the like. Whether that proves acceptable to us or not depends on how convincing he can make it, and how far we come to meet him. The scientific imagery that we shall see at work in Donne is part-personal, part-historical ; but it requires from us an understanding of his background and his thought.

A third type we can call *archetypal*, following Miss Bodkin:[2] that is, imagery of which we can only say that its persistent recurrence in all known poetry appears to be connected with some deep-rooted impulses in the unconscious which seek expression through this kind of imagery. Among them we can suggest the sun-moon relationship for male and female : the passage through a cavern as a re-birth symbol;[3] the union of a river with the sea; the complex emotions associated with forests; the relief through tears with the coming of the rain in that most strange psychological Odyssey, *The Ancient Mariner.*

There is perhaps a fourth, the so-called Freudian group, which

---

[1] But see the latest translation of the Psalms, in which the familiar version is rejected for a more accurate reading. This raises important questions of the 'habitual response'.

[2] *Archetypal Patterns in Poetry.*   [3] See (e.g.) W. H. Auden, *The Enchaféd, Flood.*

is difficult to separate from the third. I do not propose to develop this : except to state, with what emphasis I can command, my conviction that the amateur Freudian is, in literary criticism as elsewhere, the greatest danger to himself and to others. At the same time, I do not think that any critic has made a greater contribution to the understanding of poetry than Freud himself.

At this stage it is well to take stock of the position we have reached. Our poem is broken down into something like this :

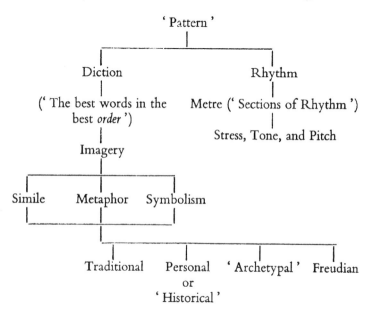

Our poem will be set in a pattern, 'P', which will be the general *shape* of the poem as well as its more complex internal organization. As simple examples :

A short lyric is frequently in the form of a circle, comprising the initial statement, a development from the statement, and a conclusion which rounds off the circle by returning to the initial point of departure.

7

A sonnet is normally an eight-six balance (between octet and sestet), with an intricately-woven rhyme-scheme.[1]

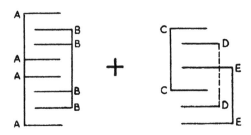

The Limerick works (in most cases) by a sort of hinge-movement in the middle : an initial statement, in the first two lines (setting the stage, as it were) : a pause on the point of balance ; and then a rapid swing-over, a dramatic reversal of the situation, going back to the first line and producing a striking situation with reference to it. Perhaps thus : You can think out your own examples.

Marvell's *To His Coy Mistress*, which is on your sheet, obviously works in three movements : thesis, antithesis, and synthesis, thus :

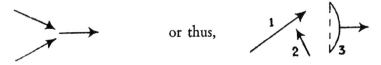

or thus,

You will notice that I have said nothing about symbolism, which I want to leave out of consideration at this stage ; suggesting only that a symbol is a multiple and complex image, related both upwards to a kind of mystical perception of reality, and downwards to a multiple series of significances. Thus, when Yeats uses one of his dominant symbols, The Tower, we

[1] This diagramatic representation stands for a normal or Petrarchan type in which the octet rhymes (invariably) ABBA ABBA. The sextet is on various permutations of two or three rhymes, though shown as CDE CDE. Consider Milton's Sonnet *On His Blindness*.

are aware (from his own repeated usages) that it has (among others) the following meanings and references :

(*a*) the poet's own remote and lonely position ;
(*b*) his ascent to that position by the winding stair—tortuously acquired experience of life ;
(*c*) the feudal Norman tower as an *obsolete* defence against the modern world ;
(*d*) various complicated personal allusions.

We shall see something of how this works in a later poem on the sheet, *The Stare's Nest by My Window*.

Yet another source of complexity in poetry is the reaction of individual words upon each other. Our response to a single line of poetry is, perhaps, comparable to a successive *re-defining* in our minds of the first meanings which we attach to each word because of what follows. In selecting the meaning we are also influenced by our previous memories, visual and otherwise, which are brought into play. We can test this readily. Close your eyes and listen to these lines from *Kubla Khan* :

> But O, that deep romantic chasm which slanted
> Down the green hill athwart a cedarn cover !
> A savage place ! as holy and enchanted
> As e'er beneath a waning moon was haunted
> By woman wailing for her demon-lover !

As you listen, you build up in stages the visual picture, modifying it at each succeeding word. The *savage spot* is changed, limited, modified or added to by *holy*, which itself is modified by *enchanted* : the scene under the waning moon changes it all again. If the image is mainly a visual one, you will re-interpret it by bringing in some memory-picture of your own : as in Tennyson's

> a sluice with blackened waters slept

or

> On one side lay the ocean, and on one
> Lay a great water, and the moon was full.

9

There is, then, an immensely complex process at work as we listen to a poem. It may, perhaps, be helpful to you if we attempt to formulate this process in algebraical terms, using some such notation as this :

Suppose a poem to consist of a certain number of words, say ' N '. We may denote these words by $W_1, W_2 \ldots W_n$. In most cases, these words will have various possible shades of meaning, and the reading of the poem will result in a progressive selection[1] of the *one or more* appropriate meanings from among these ' possibles ', in accordance with the contextual effect (including sound and rhythm) of other words in the poem ; so that, for example, we may denote the meaning of the fourth word after, say, nineteen words have been read by the symbol $M_4(19)$ or, in general that of the rth word after ' s ' have been read by $M_r^{(s)}$.

Then M_r (the final meaning) can be regarded not only as a function of W_r (its immediately corresponding word) but also of other words in the poem. Symbolically, for intermediate stages,

$$M_r^{(s)} = M_r \ (W_1, W_2, W_3 \ldots W_s).$$

As we read through the poem, i.e. as ' s ' increases, $M_r^{(s)}$ will be progressively modified by the W's until we reach the end, when it attains its final meaning M_r. We then have the final meaning of each word in its relation to all the other words in the poem, and we should then be able to perceive the pattern of the whole. We have, of course, simplified the process a little ; in certain poems, especially when we deal with symbols, we may find that one or more ' appropriate meanings ' exist simultaneously, or overlap each other, in the pattern. Further, we should think of the pattern less as a fixed framework than as a sort of biological entity growing and renewing itself as the poem progresses.

[1] It may be helpful to draw some analogy from the functioning of an automatic telephone exchange.

But there is a further complexity : the effect of sound on meaning, as apart from the pattern or rhythm. We know little about this, and our judgment on it (apart from the cruder forms of onomatopœia such as Browning's *How They Brought the Good News from Ghent to Aix*, Belloc's *Tarantella*, or Wilfred Ashley's *Goods Train at Night*), will probably be subjective. But for a simple instance on the sheet before you, consider the last stanza of *The Twa Corbies* :

> 'Mony a one for him maks mane,
> But nane sall ken whar he is gane:
> O'er his white banes, when they are bare,
> The wind sall blaw for evermair.'

Modernize the spelling ; and you have destroyed, not the rhythm, but the key of the poem: the thin high music of the lament, the endlessly subtle variations on the *a* sound, the strange feeling that all things have been unified with the shrillness of the wind through the heather.

We have mentioned the matter of subjective judgment. Because of the great complexity of the ' selector ' mechanism in our minds, and because each one of us brings to interpretation many personal memories, it seems certain that each one of us re-creates the poem for himself. Probably we re-make it to some extent on each successive reading. Part of the pleasurable excitement comes from the sense of re-creation, of making the poem for ourselves, which the poet felt at its fullest in the original act of creation. But this excitement and pleasure are closely related to our own development ; that is why Yeats revised his early work so extensively to keep in tune with his own changing set of values. He put the whole matter succinctly :

> The friends that have it I do wrong
> Whenever I remake a song
> Should know what issue is at stake :
> It is myself that I remake.

It is not to be expected, then, that we can ever 'receive' the artist's experience as he meant to transmit it: even supposing that we could know what that experience was. The process will be much more like that of a partial coincidence of a number of circles with one central circle: the diameter of the 'satellite' circles depending upon our own sensibility, the extent to which we are prepared to co-operate with the artist, and the imaginative power which we bring to interpretation. Our figure (i) will be something like this, where the shaded portion stands for the

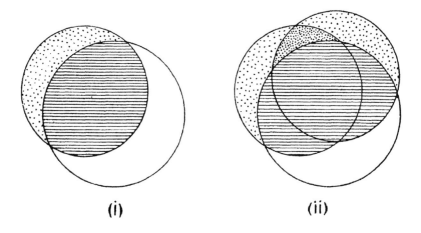

(i)   (ii)

artist's experience, as it appears in the poem ; the dotted area for what we bring in from outside, which may or may not be relevant to that experience.

The portion which is blank suggests those aspects of communication which we fail to 'receive' ; either because of failure in our own sympathy, or because his assumptions, idiom, social or historical background differ too widely from our own. In the same way, if we think of responses by two different readers we shall probably get a compound figure such as (ii), with a certain measure of coincidence between their responses, both inside and outside the area of the poet's statement, and with the peculiar and individual experiences which each will bring to the interpretation. The diagrams are exaggerated for the sake of clarity.

I spoke just now of individual or ' private ' experiences which we bring to interpretation. It is obvious that they may be illegitimate ; that is, so strong or hostile that they distort or frustrate the artist's communication. ' Ridiculous ' associations, arising out of some ambiguity, or from a parody which has been read before the original, may be of this kind. It is obvious that all associations may have to be ' censored ' before they are brought to bear upon interpretation. An extreme example of distortion (though it has, perhaps, a legitimate component) is given on page 61.

For the purpose of these lectures, we shall consider this ' criticism ' to be an art rather than a science. Because of our relatively slight knowledge of psychology and of brain-physiology, we shall get no nearer to a ' scientific ' judgment of a poem than a weighing (after due explanation) of rough ' majority ' opinions. We shall have to recognize that the complexity of our object of study, and sometimes its very intention, prohibits us from seeking to attain precision.

I say *intention*, for we shall often be concerned with ' penumbral ' statements ; which lie in a shadowy zone round the circumference of the broken light that is thrown by language. We shall find these indefinite shadowy meanings starting up when we deal, for instance, with any kind of symbolism.

It will probably be best for us to approach these poems by putting to ourselves a number of simple questions which will require very complicated answers.

(i) What is the poet trying to say ? (So far as you and I can tell.)

(ii) *How*—i.e. in what form—does he say it? for by examining his technique we shall be forced to consider meaning more closely in all its components.

13

(iii) Does he succeed in saying what we think he is trying to say ? (If not, why ? Is there a failure in technique ? Is he ' insincere ' ? [1])

(iv) Is what he has said, or is trying to say, of value or significance to the reader ?

In the last resort, these judgments of value will depend on your own philosophy. You will bring to your reading of poetry a certain set of attitudes, both emotional and mental, which you can modify, but seldom wholly escape. What you take from poetry will modify these attitudes : sometimes immediately and perceptibly, perhaps in this room ; sometimes after long periods when you have apparently forgotten it all.

[1] But this is a difficult and dangerous word, which will be discussed later.

CHAPTER II

The Ballad *The Twa Corbies*
and
Donne's *A Valediction : forbidding mourning*

I

THERE was a letter in a morning paper some time ago in which a clergyman complained that one of his wealthier parishioners had spent some three hundred pounds on his funeral ; and the writer held with some justice that the money could have been better spent on providing food for the living. And yet our instinct to live with the dead, to attribute sensation to the dead body, to ' extend our memories by monuments ', is one of the commonest. It is a mark of our own adolescence ; the description of American funeral customs in Evelyn Waugh's *The Loved One* reveals a terrifying exploitation of this instinctive emotion for commercial ends.[1] The *pompes funèbres* are commoner on the continent than here : but many of us remember seeing ' the long funerals blacken all the way ', the black horses, the *Dead March* in *Saul*, and all the dutiful respect that masked, perhaps, the truth :

> Only the dead can be forgiven:
> But when I think of that my tongue's a stone.[2]

Remember, at least, that this care for the dead body, this cushioning on satin, this sealing against decay, is as unchristian and futile as it is irrational. Sir Thomas Browne of Norwich

[1] And, more frightening because so fully documented, Jessica Mitford's *The American Way of Death.*
[2] W. B. Yeats: *A Dialogue of Self and Soul.*

summed it up in *Urn Burial* (which as scientists you should read):

> Ready to be anything in the ecstacy of being ever, and as content with six foot as the *moles* of Adrianus.

We may, perhaps, look a little deeper. Our attitude to death is of great importance in our lives. The significant provision of the moderately 'costly funeral' as a tribute to lower-class respectability is a feature of the welfare state. Death is a powerful emotional stimulant. Civilized attitudes to it are often compounded of relief disguised as sorrow, a secret and often morbid pleasure in that sorrow, a satisfaction at our own safety (' for a living dog is better than a dead lion ') and perhaps some fulfilment of our own *Todtentrieb*. Infinite reserves of emotion as well as of wealth can be expended upon our attempt to mitigate the shock to the living by expressing concern for the dead. If a normal non-morbid attitude is to be achieved, it is sometimes necessary that an astringent should clear away or lighten our own sentimental confusion. Sanity demands that the dead bury their dead; clear emotion demands that the vivid poignant sense of loss should find expression and a response in us. And we should recognize, and honour, the Christian tradition as to death. If you want to find its final expression, read the Lesson for the Burial of the Dead.[1]

With something of these thoughts in mind, and this question of a just and sane attitude to the dead, I am reading aloud to you this poem. We do not know who wrote it. It was not written down till about 1800. It is simple, artless; with metrical roughness and half-rhymes: not in the normal ballad-metre (which has a 4–3 beat) but in a 4–4 stanza. (Note that the half-rhymes are less apparent in the last two stanzas, because the rhythm quickens and grows more decisive at the end.) It is impersonal, in spite of the initial "I": no trace of individual style shows through it.

---

[1] I Cor. xv, 20–58.

As I was walking all alane,
I heard twa corbies making a mane :
The tane unto the tither did say,
' Whar sall we gang and dine the day ? '

'—In behint yon auld fail dyke
I wot there lies a new-slain knight ;
And naebody kens that he lies there
But his hawk, his hound, and his lady fair.

' His hound is to the hunting gane,
His hawk to fetch the wild-fowl hame,
His lady's ta'en anither make,
So we may mak' our dinner sweet.

' Ye'll sit on his white hause-bane,
And I'll pike out his bonny blue e'en :
Wi' ae lock o' his gowden hair
We'll theek our nest when it grows bare.

' Mony a one for him maks mane,
But nane sall ken whar he is gane :
O'er his white banes, when they are bare,
The wind sall blaw for evermair.'

It attacks, suddenly, as great poems often do. The two
ravens begin their dialogue, which is a *mane*, a complaint, a
lamentation : but for their own hunger, not for the dead
knight. The place where the knight lies is mean—*yon auld
fail dyke*—remote, lonely. But notice how *yon* gives the sense
of actuality. They have seen the body. Three living things
know where he is.

Now the hawk, hound, and lady are a kind of triple symbol
of knighthood, of gentry. Their fidelity was, or should have
been taken for granted. One of the vices of the Victorians (and
of many of us too) is to sentimentalize animals, to attribute to
them human emotions. Landseer exploits this in his pictures.
Indeed there are few more bitter experiences than to return
after absence and find that one's dog and horse no longer

remember one. (Why should this be so ?) When the ballad passed south to the sentimental English, the man who rewrote it (in bad couplets) made both hawk and hound protect their dead master ; but then he wrote

> Where shall we our breakfast take ?

instead of the fourth line. (What are the different associations of *breakfast* and *dinner* ?)

The poem moves on, hound, hawk, and lady have deserted him. The dinner is *sweet*.

> Ye'll sit on his white hause-bane,
> And I'll pike out his bonny blue e'en . . .

This unknown poet knew his stuff. Birds of prey go for the eyes of carrion first. The words are direct, vivid, economical. There is a grim contemptuous precision in the *ae lock* of the *gowden hair* ; *gowden* is a stock adjective of the ballad, but it falls surely into place here. Then follows that strange high lament in the minor key ; the wind in the heather, the bones on the moor. The dead knight is lamented—*mony an ane for him maks mane*—but it is all remote, impersonal.

I take the poem to convey a sane and wise attitude to death. There is lamentation and a bitter sense of loss : that is human and healthy. The dead body is seen for what it is ; its helplessness, the carrion of it, is given realistically, even grimly, with no attempt to sentimentalize either those that remain, or the surroundings, or his possessions that desert him. It is bare and naked, like the bones on the moor. It brings a kind of peace : and when we consider Wordsworth's ' *A slumber did my spirit seal* ' I think you should have this in mind.

Meantime, there is a certain astringent quality in some poetry which I take to be a valuable corrective to the sentimentality that is latent in most of us. I am going to read you such a one, by Thomas Hardy, himself a Victorian. It is a level bitter poem without grace of style or diction, a little awkward, like

Hardy himself. As you listen to it, think of the sentiment
lavished on pet dogs by their owners : as you know, a common
symptom of psychological incompleteness. I give it without
comment.

"Ah, are you digging on my grave
        My beloved one ?—planting rue ? "
—" No : yesterday he went to wed
One of the brightest wealth has bred.
' It cannot hurt her now,' he said,
        ' That I should not be true.' "

" Then who is digging on my grave ?
        My nearest dearest kin ? "
—" Ah, no : they sit and think, ' What use !
What good will planting flowers produce ?
No tendance of her mound can loose
        Her spirit from Death's gin.' "

" But some one digs upon my grave ?
        My enemy ?—prodding sly ? "
—" Nay : when she heard you had passed the Gate
That shuts on all flesh soon or late,
She thought you no more worth her hate,
        And cares not where you lie."

" Then, who is digging on my grave ?
        Say—since I have not guessed ! "
—" Oh it is I, my mistress dear,
Your little dog, who still lives near,
And much I hope my movements here
        Have not disturbed your rest ? "

" Ah, yes ! *You* dig upon my grave . . .
        Why flashed it not on me
That one true heart was left behind !
What feeling do we ever find
To equal among human kind
        A dog's fidelity ! "

" Mistress, I dug upon your grave
        To bury a bone, in case
I should be hungry near this spot
When passing on my daily trot.
I am sorry, but I quite forgot
        It was your resting-place."

2

A Valediction : forbidding mourning

John Donne, sometime Dean of St. Paul's, was in turn
theologian, lover, scientist, and one of the greatest preachers of
history. I have chosen this poem to show you how a great
man may use in poetry the scientific language of his day :
astronomy, theology—very much a science in their eyes—
chemistry, law, metallurgy, geometry, all enter into it. Like
many of his age, he is seeking to discover the essential unity
between different and often apparently contradictory aspects of
the universe. In the search for similarity between dissimilars
he is at liberty to bring under tribute all the scientific terminology
of his day.

Let us imagine that, on the morning of the day in which he
wrote this poem, his instrument-makers in St. Paul's Churchyard have sent him up a scientific toy ; a pair of rose-wood and
silver compasses in their velvet case. He is playing idly with
them ; now tracing the circle which is the image of God, of
Infinity, and Perfection, now easing the set-screw, which holds
the legs together, and tracing arcs at varying distances from the
centre.

There are many thoughts running in his mind. The problem
of love and its constancy is ageless. At every turn it is linked
with religion and its imagery : from the Song of Solomon
onwards through classical mythology. The poet has a quick
and clear mind ; image after image flashes across it, to be fixed

or rejected, to sharpen or dull the central problem which he is facing. And he might have reasoned thus :

" Separation from the beloved is death. That is why I am starting with the image of a dying man, with the tension of the hushed voices in the sick-room :

> As virtuous men passe mildly away,
>   And whisper to their soules, to goe,
> Whilst some of their sad friends doe say,
>   The breath goes now, and some say, no :

That is how we must part. We *melt* away. There must be no weeping ; tears and sighs are the stock-in-trade of the poets who have gone before me, and I shall deny them contemptuously. For our love has a religious ecstasy, and we are its high priests; this silence alone is fitting :

> So let us melt, and make no noise,
>   No teare-floods, nor sigh-tempests move,
> T'were prophanation of our joyes
>   To tell the layetie our love.

But floods and tempests suggest the sympathy of nature's convulsions with our parting. In every street of the City the astrologers are talking of meanings and portents ; and this is a perplexing time. But our parting is no common phenomenon. It is as if we, my love and I, were two of the celestial planets which meet and pass and separate on their orbits, and do no harm to man ; in that stately passage, they are so infinitely removed from human reckoning :

> Moving of th' earth brings harmes and feares,
>   Men reckon what it did and meant,
> But trepidation of the spheares,
>   Though greater farre, is innocent.

Then the planets suggest the moon. The moon is the female ; the symbol of change, of the ebb and flow of the tides, shedding only the reflected light from the sun, the symbol of poverty and weakness. What a terrific image it is—' Dull *sublunary* lovers love '—lovers beneath the moon and subject to its ebb and flux ! These others have no soul beyond their mere five senses. They cannot bear the thought of separation, since the senses can no longer exist apart from their fulfilment. And I shall use one word for that fusion—through sight, sound, touch, taste, and smell—the fusion, the *elementing*, as of chemicals or metals in a crucible—of all those things which in common men and women are the conditions of physical love :

> Dull sublunary lovers love
> (Whose soule is sense) cannot admit
> Absence, because it doth remove
> Those things which elemented it.

But we are different. Our love is so rare in its essence, springing from such qualities of mind and soul that physical contact is immaterial. We are certain of our minds—*inter-assured*, the heavy legal word:

> But we by a love, so much refin'd,
> That our selves know not what it is,
> Inter-assured of the mind,
> Care lesse, eyes, lips, and hands to misse.

We do not know what this love-essence is. It may be (I have written before of this) something of the nature of the aether ; [1] it may be of the nature of gold, infinitely precious, indestructible in the fire, the symbol of the soul which (I have written about this too) must be mixed with the alloy of the body before it can receive the stamp of the image in the act of procreation that makes it lawful coin.[2] So my image is gold beaten (as by the blows of suffering or separation) into the quality of air; as I have seen in the goldsmiths' shops in St. Paul's Churchyard men beat the sheet gold between the layers of skin, so that it becomes a miracle of unbroken delicacy of texture.

[1] *Aire and Angels.*   [2] *The Extasie.*

> Our two souls therefore, which are one,
>   Though I must goe, endure not yet,
> A breach, but an expansion,
>   Like gold to ayery thinnesse beate.

This is my first movement, and it links up with these quick zig-zags of thought ; death, departure, convulsions of the earth, the planets, the moon, the senses of common men, subject and bound to the body, and our own final essence, which is of the nature of an angel ; indestructible, immortal, beyond price. So—and I pick up the compasses again. This is the image which I want : two limbs, yet one instrument ; moving in harmony with each other. *Thy soule*—yes, you the woman, representing constancy in my life. You move in sympathy with my own seekings after truth, my own travels of body or of mind :

> If they be two, they are two so
>   As stiffe twin compasses are two,
> Thy soule the fixt foot, makes no show
>   To move, but doth, if the other doe.

You remain the centre of my world, and there may be yet another symbol there : for the physics of the time is just now speculating as to whether the earth may not be, under its surface layers, a kind of gigantic loadstone, drawing all things to it. Yes, I shall roam, but you are still linked to me, and in this proud symbol of a stately and noble woman greeting her husband, I will celebrate your constancy :

> And though it in the center sit,
>   Yet when the other far doth rome,
> It leanes, and hearkens after it,
>   And growes erect, as that comes home.

Yes, that is one aspect of the symbol. In absence I run my own course. I am responsible to myself alone. Yes, but that course is linked to yours, however far from you I may be. It is your constancy that ensures that, whatever my motion, I shall come back at the last to you. And the circle traced by my wanderings will be a true one; the symbol of God, of the mystery; the one mathematical form whose properties remain inscrutable, the circle which is, as it were, a component of the mystical sphere itself is the microcosm and emblem of the world:

> Such wilt thou be to mee, who must
> Like th' other foot, obliquely runne ;
> Thy firmnes drawes my circle just,
> And makes me end, where I begunne."

I need not labour the ambiguity implicit in the last lines : you will find constantly the double or triple meanings lying close beneath the surface. Instead, I quote (leaving you to draw your own inferences) a poem of Yeats' :

> O but there is wisdom
> In what the sages said ;
> But stretch that body for a while
> And lay down that head
> Till I have told the sages
> Where man is comforted.
>
> How could passion run so deep
> Had I never thought
> That the crime of being born
> Blackens all our lot ?
> But where the crime's committed
> The crime can be forgot.[1]

---

[1] *Consolation :* from *A Woman Young and Old.*

CHAPTER III

Marvell's *To His Coy Mistress*
and
Wordsworth's *A Slumber did my spirit seal*

I

IN the first lecture I referred to different structural forms of poems. The first, *The Twa Corbies*, was a straightforward progression : the second, *A Valediction*, was perhaps a circular poem, with a series of smaller satellite circles (to signify the separate images of each stanza) lying on its circumference. In the *Coy Mistress* we have more of a musical form—the statement, the anti-statement, and the resolution : three distinct movements.

Consider first the subject. It is not a mere invitation to seduction. It is, rather, a statement of man's problem when he confronts time. Time is the enemy : maybe to all poets. One view of the problem is how to embody, in a statement, the fixing of the moment to secure an apparent denial of mutability. That moment, seized on by the poet (and to be re-created at will by his reader as part of the armour against fate) is the centre of Keats' *Ode on A Grecian Urn*, where the figures of the lovers are frozen in the figures of the Urn :

> She cannot fade, though thou hast not thy bliss :
> For ever wilt thou love, and she be fair.

So Goethe's Faustus in agony :

> Werd' ich zum Augenblicke sagen :
> 'Verweile doch ! du bist so schön'!'
> Dann magst du mich in Fesseln schlagen,
> Dann will ich gern zu Grunde gehn !

25

Now the philosophy of *carpe diem* is an old one. Herrick, with his 'pretty pastoral gale of fancy', might write *Gather ye rosebuds while ye may*. (When you read that poem again think of what the imagery of the rose means—after we have read Blake's *Sick Rose* together.) But the problem that Marvell is facing is much more complex than this. Beauty vanishes, and the grave is near. What then ? What attitude of mind leads to the wisest action in relation to that knowledge ? In what scale of values may the present be set against the past and future ?

Consider the background. Marvell's family came from Melbourne, near Cambridge, and he was for seven years at Trinity College ; he was sometime Member of Parliament for Hull. He did not fight in the Civil War. He had been a Tutor to the family of Fairfax at Nunappleton House in Yorkshire. He was a diplomat, a wit, a writer. All his verse has an aristocratic spring and energy and gaiety in it : with a precision of technique that owes much (as it does in all these poets) to his classical scholarship. Now Marvell is writing at the end of the so-called metaphysical tradition. One layer farther back in time than this was the Petrarchan tradition : the poetry of rich fantastic compliment to women, which was itself a relic of the older tradition of courtly love. Like Donne—remember the *teare-floods* and *sigh-tempests* of that poem—he is hitting out at his predecessors. Perhaps as he wrote the poem he might have thought like this :

" Women have been praised long enough and extravagantly in the great Petrarchan tradition—the tradition that decorated them with the extravagance of fantastic simile, the pearls of the conceit. Yes, that is her due—for my first movement : for all poems, and all experience, grow, I think, in three movements : the Statement, the Anti-Statement, and the Synthesis.[1] Let me magnify her in this coyness: as if in that cold ecstasy of admiration all passion should be frozen into stone. ["For ever wilt thou love, and she be fair".] All right: give her the

[1] Compare the Minuet and Trio, with their ideas of Statement, Digression and Re-statement; or the Exposition, Development and Recapitulation of Sonata Form.

jewels of the Petrarchan Sonnet ; the great Italianate tradition, as of those Elizabethan women, so arrogant with their calm white faces, so stiff in the defence of the stomacher and embroidered gown——

> Had we but World enough, and Time,
> This coyness Lady were no crime.

—Yes, time must be the keynote of the poem : she has lost her sense of reality, secure in her own admiration. All right—give her more :

> —We would sit down, and think which way
> To walk, and pass our long Loves Day.

We like gardens : the pleached formal gardens of the seventeenth century, every tree and bed a parable of order : we can look into each other's eyes (as Donne and the great lovers did) and all the yearning of desire is in those liquid l's—*long Loves Day*. But—on with the decoration of the Renaissance :

> Thou by the *Indian Ganges'* side
> Should'st Rubies find—[1]

—glittering with them in the hot sunlight : build up the contrast of our separation in climate and time, brightness of light against my own grey river—

> —Should'st Rubies find : I by the Tide
> Of *Humber* would complain.

Yes, that's it ; the traditional Lover, pining through eternity : lay the paint on heavier, with all the extravagance of proverb and tradition.

> —I would
> Love you ten years before the Flood—

Good, that *ten years*—the arrogance of that precision of time pin-pointed in eternity !

> —And you should if you please refuse
> Till the Conversion of the *Jews*.

[1] There may be an oblique allusion, between irony and compliment, from Proverbs 31, 10: 'Who can find a virtuous woman? for her price is far above rubies.'

(That is, of course, for ever.)

> My vegetable Love should-grow
> Vaster than Empires, and more slow.

That's good, too : *vegetable*, with the beat hanging heavy on it, conveys a paradox in its qualifying of *Love*—which is, of course, all fire and air in its purity ; but *I* want to suggest this slow half-sentient growth of love, which has all eternity before it. Now bring her nearer to the painted cloth of tradition. Every part of her must be glorified, as the body of a saint—

> An hundred years should go to praise
> Thine Eyes, and on thy Forehead Gaze.
> Two hundred to adore each Breast :
> But thirty thousand to the rest.
> An Age at least to every part,
> And the last Age should show your Heart.
> For Lady you deserve this State ;
> Nor would I love at lower rate.

So. That's the background, and the first movement of the symphony ; and I meant those last two lines ; for my passion is rising with the rhythm of ordered words. How incomparable she is ! And there are moods in which a Lover knows that suspension of time, and just that yearning for its continuance : that slow exploration of all attributes and beauty, of spirit and of body.

But—many men have written thus : and most of them have stopped just there. That will leave her in her dream world, the stiff brocaded portrait of virginity, full of false pride. Now we'll turn on her, and show her what is behind this adoring make-believe world :

> But at my back I alwaies hear
> Times winged Charriot hurrying near [1]

---

[1] Note how the rolling double r's of *Charriot* quicken and shorten the word and carry over to *hurrying*. I have used here the text (in the main) from Grierson's *Metaphysical Poetry*. Much is gained in weight by the capitals of the names. The more familiar version, as in *The Oxford Book of English Verse*, is given at Appendix I.

That's it—that gives what I mean: the words are moving now in my mind. "At my back"—aren't we all haunted, afraid to look behind?[1] The chariot—the horsemen—the fear of the armour and the archetypal might of the horses, the wings both for speed and for the god-like quality of time, and the quick beat of the horse-hoofs in those short syllables, growing louder as they drive on—

—Charriot hurrying near :

Remember that image in the Bible—the chariot, the armoured troops, the Philistines, that have become the symbol of fear ? ' Some put their trust in chariots and some in horses, but we will remember the name of the Lord.' And then ? Do we go out cold into the dark ; or is it the crossing of the Dark River ; or is it, as I think, just emptiness, as of a nightmare, sandy waste (listen to the *a* of *desarts*) and the pitiful souls who must traverse eternity alone?—And yonder all before us lye
Desarts of vast Eternity.

Well, my Mistress—what about the eyes, and the lips, and the breasts then ?

—Thy Beauty shall no more be found ;
Nor in thy marble Vault, shall sound
My ecchoing Song. . . .

Yes, I know you'll have a marble vault, and Latin to extol your virtues—

' Not marble, nor the gilded monuments
Of princes, shall outlive this powerful rime—'[2]

while you turn to corruption. And you'll like to believe all the rubbish about your becoming immortal in my poetry—it would echo there in that cold emptiness, wouldn't it ? Yes, I know the poets have said it—Ronsard and the rest—but it's

[1] Consider *The Ancient Mariner*, l. 451.   [2] Shakespeare's *Sonnets*, lv.

29

wrong, wrong. You listen : we'll consider this tomb a little more closely. (You've been cruel—I can be cruel too.)

> . . . then worms shall try
> That *long preserv'd* Virginity . . .

Have you seen the ambiguity of that tiny word *try* ? It is not merely the sexual word for the horrible consummation ; it is the scientific word, the metallurgical word, for the assaying of purity.

> 'For as pure gold is *tried* in the furnace' . . .

Preserved by your coyness for this—this—can't you feel the slow horror of that marriage ? Shakespeare knew it, with Juliet, the girl-bride's fear—

> Or shut me nightly in a charnel-house,
> O'er-cover'd quite with dead men's rattling bones,
> With reeky shanks, and yellow chapless skulls . . . [1]

John Donne drew the trail of the worm across a hundred poems and sermons. And then ? . . .

> And your quaint Honour turn to dust ;
> And into ashes all my Lust—

Quaint Honour—see how the beats fall heavy upon it. For, when you face the tomb, you will see things in scale again : and this fantasy of yours to preserve a worthless virginity—O yes, I can be cruel to myself too—my lust goes with your honour—but then *I* have no illusions. Other men have written of the lovers in a single grave, and roses growing from them : and the living love to sentimentalize on their own forgiveness of the dead. I know they talk of the Grave and the Bed ; Shakespeare did ; Death the Lover, the Bride and the Bridegroom : but—I know, and you must too

> —The Grave's a fine and private place,
> But none I think, . . .

---

[1] *Romeo and Juliet*, iv, 1.

—take that very slowly, and quietly, to bring out that arrogance that denies a whole poetic tradition, past and to come :

> But none I think do there embrace."

(So the second movement ends. The lesser man might have stopped at the end of the first, or here : he might have left us depressed, or with a cynicism of fear, or with the morbid sentimentality of romanticism. Listen to Tennyson —though, to do him justice, *Maud* is a study of an adolescent hysteria:

> She is coming, my own, my sweet ;
>   Were it ever so airy a tread,
> My dust would hear her and beat,
>   Were it earth in an earthy bed ;
> My dust would hear her and beat,
>   Had I lain for a century dead ;
> Would start and tremble under her feet,
>   And blossom in purple and red.

There we are getting into queer country. Don't laugh at this absurdity. Remember *Hamlet* :

> I do know
> When the blood burns, how prodigal the soul
> Lends the tongue vows. [1]

But this man is greater. He has seen it all—both sides of the picture—the Idea and the Reality. And then, with the gay insolence of the cavalier, and the passionate intellectual power of the metaphysical, the whole conflict is resolved.)

"All right—we accept the tomb. And once we accept it, and stop idealizing our love and you—then it is all made clear again. This is our triumph : and with it the verse will quicken as the pulse quickens, and the remote picture poem becomes flesh and blood again. Yes, she is lovely—with rich bloom—

---

[1] *Hamlet*, i, 3.

the 'lew' (a forgotten word) [1]—the soft delicate haze which the mist makes on the landscape early on a summer morning : with the texture and bloom and scent of the cheeks of a woman who is young, and happy, and in love, and who has been brought out of the captivity of a dream.

> Now, therefore, while the youthful hew
> Sits on thy skin like morning lew,
> And while thy willing Soul transpires
> At every pore with instant Fires—

Yes, I've torn down your mask, my Dear ; you can't wear it any more. It was only a pose.

> Now let us sport us while we may
> And now, like am'rous birds of prey
> Rather at once our Time devour
> Than languish in his slow-chapt pow'r.

Good, that—*am'rous birds of prey*. You see, I wanted to show the ferocity, and the cruelty, and pride, and above all the triumphant sense of *riding* down the world in our strength, like eagles, now that we've ceased to be afraid of Time. For we can control him, so long as we do not fear. Eat, or be eaten— slow jaws moving, gnawing—didn't Ronsard write about that ?

> —Ce qu'a rongé le temps injurieux—

We—we are the masters of time, and of the world : we *are* the world, our passion is a microcosm of it : we are the mystic Sphere which is eternity. Male and female—strength and sweetness—meet in it :

> Let us roll all our Strength, and all
> Our sweetness up into one Ball,
> And tear our pleasures with rough strife,
> Thorough the Iron gates of Life—

---

[1] I have taken this textual emendation instead of the familiar *dew*. " Lew is the heat-haze, the ' bloom ' which the dew makes on the landscape early in a warm day, and this transient, warm bloom is compared with the *duveté* of his mistress' complexion : something very delicate, shown only in a peculiar light or a particular posture " (*Andrew Marvell*, M. C. Bradbrook and M. G. Lloyd Thomas)

We shall *tear* it—like the eagles I was thinking of just now : rough strife, my dear, for love is not a matter of listening to sonnets to your forehead, but of your own fierce creative act of love-making, as of eagles, in their strength and splendour. Out, outside those gates—*iron* that clangs in the line,[1] like the gates of hell—or of that marble vault : *iron* that is bitter, and a prison, and a wound, to man or to God. We have conquered : and with one last gesture, and the gaiety of giants, I fling out the challenge in a last splendid paradox. The fight is on between us two in our love ; and between us and Time, for we have conquered him and his threat of an unmoving world, the world of the dream or of the tomb. We cannot bid the sun stand still, as Joshua did, upon Gibeon : or still the progress of the earth, as Zeus did, while we take joy of our love. But we know that our strength and energy is released in harmony with Time, who is now fleeing from us—or with us—in the great motion of the world . . .

> Thus, though we cannot make our Sun
> Stand still, yet we will make him run."

2

A Slumber did my spirit seal

This is the last poem of a sequence known as the Lucy Poems, written by Wordsworth in 1799. They celebrate a dead girl. So that you may see her more clearly, I am going to read you first the poem that precedes it in the sequence :

> Three years she grew in sun and shower,
> Then Nature said, " A lovelier flower
> On earth was never sown ;
> This Child I to myself will take ;
> She shall be mine, and I will make
> A Lady of my own.

---

[1] I would have it spelt and pronounced *yron*, so as to bring out the roll of the *r*.

" Myself will to my darling be
Both law and impulse : and with me
The Girl, in rock and plain,
In earth and heaven, in glade and bower,
Shall feel an overseeing power
To kindle or restrain.

" She shall be sportive as the Fawn
That wild with glee across the lawn
Or up the mountain springs ;
And hers shall be the breathing balm,
And hers the silence and the calm
Of mute insensate things.

" The floating Clouds their state shall lend
To her ; for her the willow bend ;
Nor shall she fail to see
Even in the˙motions of the Storm
Grace that shall mould the Maiden's form
By silent sympathy.

" The stars of midnight shall be dear
To her ; and she shall lean her ear
In many a sacred place
Where Rivulets dance their wayward round,
And beauty born of murmuring sound
Shall pass into her face.

" And vital feelings of delight
Shall rear her form to stately height,
Her virgin bosom swell ;
Such thoughts to Lucy will I give
While she and I together live
Here in this happy Dell."

Thus Nature spake—The work was done—
How soon my Lucy's race was run !
She died, and left to me
This heath, this calm, and quiet scene ;
The memory of what has been,
And never more will be.

The girl has grown up with nature ; she has drawn joy, and strength, and power from the mountains and the woods. (That is Wordsworth's great legacy to us, the final and perfect expression of his experience of

> a sense sublime
> Of something far more deeply interfused,
> Whose dwelling is the light of setting suns . . .
> A motion and a spirit, that impels
> All thinking things, all objects of all thought,
> And rolls through all things.) [1]

Sometimes, in the perverse cycles of popular taste, you will find people who laugh at Wordsworth. Take no heed of them. Most of us still return to mountains and the sea to get strength and peace of mind; more than ever now, as life grows noisier and faster. (Arnold put it well in praise of Wordsworth:

> He laid us as we lay at birth
> On the cool flowery lap of earth ;
> Smiles broke from us, and we had ease.
> The hills were round us, and the breeze
> Went o'er the sun-lit fields again :
> Our foreheads felt the wind and rain.
> Our youth return'd : for there was shed
> On spirits that had long been dead,
> Spirits dried up and closely-furl'd,
> The freshness of the early world.) [2]

And now the girl is dead, and the poet is considering all that he has lost. It is a tiny poem, with complete simplicity of diction : only one word, Latin and cosmic, comes into it with a kind of resonance. Listen :

> A Slumber did my spirit seal ;
> I had no human fears :
> She seemed a thing that could not feel
> The touch of earthly years.

---

[1] *Tintern Abbey.*   [2] *Memorial Verses.*

> No motion has she now, no force ;
> She neither hears nor sees,
> Rolled round in earth's diurnal course,
> With rocks, and stones, and trees.

The strange thing about this poem is that it seems to include something unspoken : that lies, as it were, *between* the two verses. Consider the first. It is highly complex, with a suggestion of a trance effect ;

> A Slumber did my spirit seal

as in the past he had been isolated, numbed in his consciousness. The word *seal* is strange; suggesting, perhaps, secrecy, isolation.[1] Notice how the vowels are modulated, how the sibilant s's seem to quicken the line till the clenching of it on the final word. In the next line—

> I had no human fears

the fourth word seems to carry a slightly heavier stress : *human* contrasted with *spirit*.

> She seemed a thing—

—a *thing*, almost inanimate, as if the poet is watching her from a distance ; it is as if she possessed a statuesque quality, to be preserved and cherished, inviolable by time. Against this the word *touch* comes almost with a shock : though it is a complex word, suggesting both tenderness, lightness, and (in the context) something inexorable too. And the touch of *earthly* years closes up the word-ranks of the stanza : *earthly, human, spirit*.

She dies, and there is a pause while the full implications of the event grow in the poet's mind. We have moved from the past into the present. There is no *seeming* ; the girl is dead. The world of nature remains, and she is identified with it. Between the two stanzas there is, unspoken, the poet's knowledge of his loss. The first verse was secure, almost arrogant in security. In the interval he has had to reconsider all his values, all that his *sealed* spirit had turned away. And the emotion in the last

[1] Perhaps, too, elation: v. *Revelations*

36

stanza seems to me to be capable of interpretation in two ways. (Great poetry often does just this thing : perhaps giving back, like a mirror, the mood of the reader.) From one point of view it is a cry of pain ; pain under great control ; reticent in its understatement, for it is thus that great literature conveys in simplicity its moments of the utmost tension. In another mood I find in it an acceptance, a humility as contrasted with the earlier arrogance. The world of nature remains, and she is absorbed into it. In order that this absorption, this fusion, may be stated more fully, the cosmic motion of the globe is emphasized :

Rolled round in earth's diurnal course

Diurnal—the heavy latinized word, carrying the main stress of the line, suggests the remorseless unending motion of the universe. (Many poets have used, for some such purpose as this, the Latin-rooted words that lie deep in our consciousness. Remember that, till recently, Latin was the speech of all science, philosophy, theology. It brings out of the past an accumulated seriousness that no other language can give.)

She dies, and is *rolled round*, in peace or in helpless passivity, as you will, with rocks and stones and trees. Perhaps this is subjective, but I find in these three words a progressive lightening, as it were, of the tension. The rock is to me the menacing, the oppressive thing ; stones are smaller, less hostile, but still, in the language of imagery, dead and cold ; trees, by contrast, suggest deep-rooted solidity, and yet a life unified with earth and sky. Perhaps it is for this reason that I feel this sense of resignation, of acceptance, of the exchange of one kind of life for a different kind, of absorption into the body of the universe.

You remember *The Twa Corbies* of the second lecture. Here are two ways of looking at death : the dead knight in the heather, and the girl who is again joined to the rhythm of the universe from which she took her life and vitality. There is no morbidity, nothing to terrify or oppress. The statements in both poems seem to me to be worth your consideration.

CHAPTER IV

Two kinds of obscurity :
Blake's *The Sick Rose* : and a passage from
T. S. Eliot's *The Waste Land*

I

TO-DAY I am going to ask you to consider some aspects of symbolism. We take our symbol—the rose, the tower, the lily, the moon—and allow it to suggest, both by its contextual usage, and by the pattern in which it is set, a series of indeterminate ' penumbral ' meanings ; which are on the borderline of thought and feeling, which cannot be expressed, or hinted at, in any other way ; and which are justified precisely by their indeterminacy. When we deal with a symbol, it is rather as if we drew the cork from the magic bottle of the Arabian Nights. First a kind of thick and confusing smoke pours out ; then strange forms take shape out of the smoke, and modify each other, perpetually shifting in the corners of our mind.

So with this poem of Blake's. Before I read it aloud I will tell you of the engraving Blake made to illustrate it : or rather, the illustration he conceived *with* the poem, for the two are inextricably blended. (It is so with nearly all Blake's poems : you must take them with the engravings.)

You must imagine, then, a drawing of two briar shoots with vicious hooked thorns, that start in the left-hand side of the picture, curve round the top, and return down the left-hand side, to end in a drooping, battered rose. On the stem of one briar, in the top left-hand corner, you can just see a caterpillar, eating a leaf. From the centre of the rose itself the tiny naked

BLAKE: *The Sick Rose*

figure of a woman is leaping, as it were, with arms outstretched : underneath her, a kind of tongue or tube, suggesting a worm. Whether it is entering the rose, or leaving it, we cannot tell for certain. The other briar stem has several side shoots. On the lower one is a kneeling figure, her hair falling over her face and to the ground as if she were mourning. On the upper, a male figure, half-naked, half-dressed in a priest's garment, lies along the briar and its thorns. In the space between the briars and the rose-blossom the poem is engraved. Here it is :

O Rose, thou art sick !
The invisible worm,
That flies in the night,
In the howling storm,

Has found out thy bed
Of crimson joy ;
And his dark secret love
Does thy life destroy.

Now let us consider first the data that we already have. First there is what we may call our standard symbolism : the *rose* is woman, the *worm* is the male principle, or sex, or lust : the *storm* is obviously a conflict of some kind, standing for what is erratic, uncontrolled, destructive, whether in thought or action. Thorns stand for cruelty, oppression ; the source is obvious. Crimson is the colour of passion, blood, royalty.

We must now turn to Blake's drawing, and take from it what clues we can. The caterpillar is lust ; we know that from Shakespeare. It may also be any kind of parasitical, destructive thing. The priest and his meaning are more difficult, but we remember another couplet of Blake's :

And priests in black gowns were walking their rounds,
And binding with briars my joys and desires.

The weeping woman is no more than a kind of chorus : the female soul weeping for her sister in her death. The naked

39

woman leaping from the heart of the rose is the spirit of joy departing from it. She looks rather like a figure from one of Blake's illustrations to Milton's *L'Allegro*. The worm that is entering the rose is that which has caused her sickness and which has driven out joy.

Now with all this in mind, read the poem again ; but do *not* try to fix logical meanings for each symbol. Let them remain free, as it were, to react upon each other, to form a pattern, however indistinct it may be at this stage. (Remember that you may not begin to understand fully for ten years, or twenty.)

As you re-read it something like this may emerge, as nearly as we can find words to express what is beyond expression :

" Womanhood, the rose, is sick ; the spirit of joy has left her. She has been attacked or raped, unnaturally (in the howling storm) by lust, itself contrary to nature and joy. The flying worm is perhaps the dragon (consider all the mythological stories connected with the rescue from the dragon). The lust principle (here the engraving comes in) is parasitical, selfish (the caterpillar). It has become what it is, unnatural and destructive, because of the briars of religious prohibitions."

That is perhaps one layer of meaning. It may be that there are several more. These may exist simultaneously with each other ; but (and this is important) they may be in apparent contradiction of each other, and yet be valid. Much poetry, and religion, is paradoxical in its essence ; as if our moving point of truth, ' T ', lay outside and above two irreconcilable opposites, and could only be apprehended, but never comprehended, by bringing those opposites into a kind of compressed or accelerated relationship. So, for example, the paradox " Whosoever would save his life shall lose it " : and Blake's own series of paradoxes, such as " The road of excess leads to the palace of wisdom ", or (still more obscure) " Damn braces ; Bless relaxes."

Among the paradoxical meanings of *The Sick Rose* there may

be an invitation to ponder the paradox of death and birth, love bringing death, the sacrifice of the mother to the child ; something of which Oscar Wilde meant when he wrote

> For each man kills the thing he loves . . .[1]

The subject is a mystery. We know from other poems that the thought was perpetually fermenting in Blake's mind:

> My Mother groan'd, my Father wept ;
> Into a dangerous world I leapt ;
> Helpless, naked, piping loud,
> Like a fiend hid in a cloud.

There are other thoughts latent in this poem : and here I would speak to you of an infallible test for all great art, whether pictures, buildings, music, literature. The great things have this strange power of giving off, as it were, a continuous *radiation* of meaning : changing, probably, in relation to men and their civilizations, but always regenerating themselves in some magical way. No great building is ever twice the same ; it changes perpetually with light and atmosphere, and its harmonies are so complex that no one of us can ever absorb them all. So with poetry, and all its images and symbols.

And here is a curious thing. You or I may be deceived, for a short time, by the specious or empty thing, and prefer it above that which does not show its qualities at first. But go back to each repeatedly ; and then you will find that the lesser thing dwindles till its emptiness is apparent, while the greater unfolds quality after quality within its own living organism. The truth is, of course, that few of us have the leisure to apply the time-test in this way ; we all read too much, too rapidly, and learn to forget what we read in order to defend ourselves against the mass of paper that overwhelms us, and will, maybe, end us.

[1] *The Ballad of Reading Gaol.*

It is my intention in this lecture to discuss with you two kinds of obscurity in poetry. The Blake poem involved what we might call mystical symbolism, though in a fairly simple form. The second example is taken from T. S. Eliot's *The Waste Land,* a poem of immense importance as a social document of the first post-war period, the 1920's, and as an example of Eliot's peculiar technique. Many of you have read a good deal of him already and he remains, I suppose, with Yeats, the most important figure in English poetry for the past century or so.

It is possible to explain in outline the working of ' allusive ' poetry. All great poets use it to a greater or less extent ; as Milton with his vast learning and his complicated system of references through the use of proper names ; or with him, and countless other poets, the perpetual use of mythology, in some form or other. Now a poet is always looking out for means by which he can extend his range of expression, through new words, new rhythms, new patterns. The same quest is proper to any artist. The poet is faced with special difficulties. The supply of new words is limited, and they are absorbed relatively slowly into a language. He can make new words, without running too much risk of becoming incomprehensible, by using double-epithets, as Milton and Keats did; by using more violently-yoked compounds, as Hopkins did; or even by experimenting with a kind of new speech, relying on the sound-values of portions of known words, welded or fused together, like Gertrude Stein or James Joyce.

Another way of obtaining extensions of meaning is to use previous poetry (though all poets do this more or less) and to lift out words or phrases or lines *together with the meaning which surrounded them in their previous context* and to re-set them, as it were, in a new context. We then get highly complex results, obtainable in no other way.

Consider it thus. In the passage before you there are direct allusions to, or quotations from, Spenser, the Psalms, Andrew Marvell, Aeschylus, an obscure Australian ballad, and so forth. Suppose we call these A_1, A_2, and so on. Let R_1, R_2, etc. denote the original response of the reader to that part of the poem which the quoted line or phrase evokes, or reaches in our memory. Then, using the notation of Chapter I for words (W) and their meanings (M), we see that M_r now depends upon three variables, namely W_r (its immediately corresponding word), secondly the effect of W_1, W_2, $W_3 \ldots W_n$ (the remaining words of the poem) ; and finally R_r, the particular response evoked by an allusion A_r ; or, symbolically,

$$M_r^{(s)} = M_r\,(W_1,\,W_2,\,W_3 \ldots W_s)$$
$$+\,R_r(A_1,\,A_2,\,A_3 \ldots A_s)$$

as the response to the ' allusive ' lines or phrase modifies the meaning, not only of the words in their immediate setting, *but of the whole pattern* of the poem ; and the response to the allusion will itself be modified by its setting in the poem. The net effect is to make possible an enormous range of effects, through a sort of counter-pointing of two types of response : that engendered by the poem as it progresses, set against that evoked from another context, and each modifying the other.

Now look at this extract from *The Fire Sermon*. After reading it through as a whole, we can try to establish some of the contrapuntal effects.

The river's tent is broken : the last fingers of leaf
Clutch and sink into the wet bank. The wind
Crosses the brown land, unheard. The nymphs are departed.
Sweet Thames, run softly, till I end my song.
The river bears no empty bottles, sandwich papers,
Silk handkerchiefs, cardboard boxes, cigarette ends
Or other testimony of summer nights. The nymphs are departed.
And their friends, the loitering heirs of city directors,
Departed, have left no addresses.
By the waters of Leman I sat down and wept . . .

Sweet Thames, run softly till I end my song,
Sweet Thames, run softly, for I speak not loud or long.
But at my back in a cold blast I hear
The rattle of the bones, and chuckle spread from ear to ear.

A rat crept softly through the vegetation
Dragging its slimy belly on the bank
While I was fishing in the dull canal
On a winter evening round behind the gashouse
Musing upon the king my brother's wreck
And on the king my father's death before him.
White bodies naked on the low damp ground
And bones cast in a little low dry garret,
Rattled by the rat's foot only, year to year.
But at my back from time to time I hear
The sound of horns and motors, which shall bring
Sweeney to Mrs. Porter in the spring.
O the moon shone bright on Mrs. Porter
And on her daughter
They wash their feet in soda water
Et O ces voix d'enfants, chantant dans la coupole !

Twit twit twit
Jug jug jug jug jug jug
So rudely forc'd.
Tereu

Unreal City
Under the brown fog of a winter noon
Mr. Eugenides, the Smyrna merchant
Unshaven, with a pocket full of currants
C.i.f. London : documents at sight,
Asked me in demotic French
To luncheon at the Cannon Street Hotel
Followed by a weekend at the Metropole.

Take the third and fourth lines :

                  The nymphs are departed.
      Sweet Thames, run softly till I end my song.

The ambiguity of *nymphs* is obvious ; the term from pastoral poetry recalling all its delicacy and grace, and the same term used at times by the eighteenth century for ladies of the town. The next line is the refrain from Spenser's great *Prothalamion*, the song before a girl's marriage, stately and delicate ; and the immediate irony is apparent in its effect on the *nymphs*, and the description in the next three lines of the Thames after a party. Notice how the flat prose rhythms deny and contrast with the leap and spring of Spenser's line. A little later we have the parody, as it were, of the Psalm that describes the years in exile : *By the waters of Babylon we sat down and wept : when we remembered thee, O Sion.* But now it is the waters of Leman—Leman Street in Whitechapel, with the black oily river running beside : and Leman is also Elizabethan English for a lover. *By the waters of Leman. . . .* Then we link up again with Spenser, and the repeated quotation takes on a new significance. *But at my back . . .* you will have picked up already from Marvell's *To His Coy Mistress*

> But at my back I alwaies hear . . .

which is repeated further on. Sweeney is a lay character that Eliot uses. Mrs. Porter and her daughter are taken from an Australian Ballad. But the episode is complicated by being a half parody of an obscure Elizabethan poem, Day's *Parliament of Bees* :

> When of the sudden, listening, you shall hear
> A sound of horns and hunting, which shall bring
> Actaeon to Diana in the spring
> Where all shall see her naked skin . . .[1]

I need not labour the parallels : but you can now see something of the complicated texture which Eliot produces in order to convey attitudes which are outside the reach of simple statement.

In the next division of the poem there is an imitation of the song of the nightingale—more counter-pointing of attitudes—

[1] See, for a detailed exposition, F. O. Matthiessen, *The Achievement of T. S. Eliot.*

and the allusion to the legend of her rape.[1]   Then, suddenly comes Mr. Eugenides, the Smyrna merchant, linked both to the City directors and to the nightingales of Greece ; carrying samples of his wares (carriage and insurance free) in his pocket : part of the unreal city, the empty values, the parody of all that was noble in the Elizabethan world.

There is much else that we might emphasize : the repetition of the word *brown*, of autumn (the denial of fertility) and decay : the use of the word *clutch*—the fingers clutch—suggestive of drowning fingers ; the allusion to the washing of the feet, which I need not labour ; the figure of Tiresias (which comes later in the poem) musing *upon the king my brother's wreck*, the mysterious figure that foreshortens time, and mingles past and present.

3

And now you are asking : ' If poetry is to be as difficult and involved as this, if it demands so much study and research, if the poet himself feels that he must write notes upon his meaning, or refer us to other books as Eliot refers us to Jessie Weston's *From Ritual to Romance*—is it really worth the effort ?   Can't modern poetry be simpler than this ?   We haven't time to ferret out all these obscurities ; even if they are valuable and important, which we're inclined to doubt.'

The answers to those questions may be a little involved.   In the first instance, I quote to you this, believing it to be in the main true for this age: "We are exasperated by poetry that we do not understand, and contemptuous of poetry that we understand without effort." I doubt whether great poetry which is completely simple, in the sense that, say, most of Wordsworth's is, can ever be written again.

For these last two decades most poetry has been concerned

---

[1] Philomela was betrayed by Tereus—hence *Tereu*—who cut out her tongue. She was afterwards changed into a nightingale.

to echo or to 'imitate' the convolutions of the modern mind in its uncertainties. To do this it relies largely on taking up the past, examining it, setting it against the present. Language, as I said earlier, has not kept pace with the human mind. Symbolism has only a limited appeal, and demands a considerable background before you can receive much from its statements. I think there must always be effort in reading and understanding almost all poetry; and certainly two-thirds of modern poetry. Some people will tell you that you need not explore these ramifications of meaning, that you can merely listen to the poetry and the meaning will then suggest itself to you. I do not believe this. Neither Milton nor Eliot gives full value to the superficial reader, though for different reasons. Milton and his readers shared a common culture, and a background of the classics that you and I lack, and can only recapture through notes. That knowledge made him free of a kind of shorthand that put at his disposal all known history and mythology, with its complex overtones and allusions. When he wrote, of Satan reviewing the troops of hell,

> and what resounds
> In fable or romance of Uther's son,
> Begirt with British and Armoric knights;
> And all who since, baptiz'd or infidel,
> Jousted in Aspramont or Montalban,
> Damasco, or Marocco, or Trebisond;
> Or whom Biserta sent from Afric shore
> When Charlemain with all his peerage fell
> By Fontarabbia. . . .[1]

we wonder at the sound of the names, and something of their pageantry gets across to us.

> (Though I know no Greek, I love the sound of it;
> It goes so thundering as though it conjured devils.)

Perhaps we even know, vaguely, something of Charlemagne. But most of us do not know till we have looked into them that

[1] *Paradise Lost*, I, p. 579.

47

the names catch up, as it were, all the most famous wars of legend and history : and that they lead us round the Mediterranean and sometimes France in the great series of battles that saved Christendom from the Turk. No less accumulated traditions of courage and strength could have served to convey Milton's vision of Satan's troops. We are too near the time, or maybe the values are too indeterminate, to think of similar values being found in Dieppe or Anzio or Arnhem, or Hell-Fire Corner, and as being one day set in metre; though the issues were perhaps greater than at Roncesvalles.

Milton's learning, Donne's scientific language, Shakespeare's often intricate allusions to hunting and hawking, all demand a study no different in kind from that required for Eliot or Yeats. You will get something from the verse even if you cannot take the trouble to read closely; but you will get only a small fraction of the richness that is there. You will have missed the intellectual pleasure of exploration, and (far more important) you will have missed all the growing stimulus to your imagination, all the fermentation, as it were, set up by these complexities, that seems to continue outside and beyond the poem; much as a good play goes on working outside the theatre.

As to whether the labour is worth while, that is for you to judge. It is a vulgar error of the worst kind to suppose that the experience which we call aesthetic can ever be achieved easily in any art : music, painting, architecture, sculpture. Each one of them demands care and study ; and what is still more vital, a perpetual excitement in exploration, and the certainty that you can never come to the end. Yet, until we do, we are in no position to say whether it is ' worth while '.

CHAPTER V

Two Poems by Yeats :
The Stare's Nest by my Window
and
Before the World was Made

I

THESE two poems will seem to you, perhaps, a strange choice. But I have chosen them for definite reasons, and not merely because I take Yeats to be one of the greatest of modern poets. Each poem provides, in a different way, types of experience which can be related quickly and easily to ' normal ' experiences in war or love ; that is, they embody a factor of ' recognition ' —" Ah, that is he ! "—in war and love.

The first one seems to me to be a kind of microcosmic representation of the reactions of a poet to one aspect of war. It refers to the Irish ' Troubles ' which smouldered on intermittently from the 1916 Rising in Ireland well on into the middle 1920's. Yeats did not fight. By 1920 he was a man of fifty-five. He had just bought for a few pounds a ruined Norman castle, with a cottage beside, on the borders of Clare and Galway. He had brought to it his bride, and his daughter was born there. Now to most of us the wars we have seen have been too vast in scale to be capable of being apprehended as a whole. You and I have had our isolated experiences, fragmentary in their nature ; on the periphery, as it were, of war. This Irish Rising, and the ' Troubles ', were on a comparatively tiny scale : it was ' perspicuous ' to a poet. It made sense ; it was a war

49

started in the old tradition with a definite objective ; it was not engineered in the seemingly casual manner of the last two wars, initiated by a remote assassination or by a dictator's exhausted patience. In the midst of it was a poet—who half-believed that he had started that war.

Before I read it aloud, here are the meanings that I attach (perhaps wrongly) to the symbols used. *Stare*, incidentally, is Irish, and Elizabethan English, for starling. The bee may be taken at first simply as a symbol of wisdom, industry. (Honey often stands for wisdom, too.) The *wall* stands for security, protection : whether of a way of life, or of the poet's own personality. I think the phrase *house of the stare* is not a periphrasis for nest, but a kind of assertion of the *dynastic* quality, as it were, of the bird (' No hungry generations tread thee down '). The other thing I want you to notice is the refrain ; which is the same for each verse, yet which changes its meaning, in some strange manner, with each verse. (Remember what I said in the first lecture about the way in which words *interact* continually upon each other. The same is true of lines and of even larger units.)

> The bees build in the crevices
> Of loosening masonry, and there
> The mother birds bring grubs and flies.
> My wall is loosening ; honey-bees,
> Come build in the empty house of the stare.
>
> We are closed in, and the key is turned
> On our uncertainty ; somewhere
> A man is killed, or a house burned,
> Yet no clear fact to be discerned :
> Come build in the empty house of the stare.
>
> A barricade of stone or of wood ;
> Some·fourteen days of civil war ;
> Last night they trundled down the road
> That dead young soldier in his blood :
> Come build in the empty house of the stare

We had fed the heart on fantasies,
The heart's grown brutal from the fare ;
More substance in our enmities
Than in our love ; O honey-bees,
Come build in the empty house of the stare.

The first verse is in part a statement that is oblique to the poem : that is, its relevance is not immediately apparent. It is an invocation ; wisdom, and the slow industry of nature, is invited to enter as the defences of Self decay. The poet's wall is loosening, and yet he is *closed in*, locked in uncertainty by some external force. Nothing struck me more, in that line, than its truth to one's feeling of helpless ignorance then : roads were blockaded, bridges broken down, all telegraph wires cut. Rumour, full of tongues, was everywhere. Notice the casual flat tone that Yeats uses deliberately

> somewhere
> A man is killed, or a house burned

And then the refrain comes in with its new meaning : this time, I fancy, one of hopeless, weary contempt, of impatience at the whole business.

In the next verse two rapid lines, also handled with apparent carelessness, outline the picture : flat, economical, precise words, with a sense of actuality, of having been there, from the *fourteen days of civil war*. And this impression is accentuated by *Last night*, with the word *trundled*—the familiar, humdrum word, of a handcart or a wheelbarrow, and conveying perfectly the slackness, the insignificance, of the dead body. (Remember Hamlet's

> I'll *lug* the *guts* into the neighbour room.)

And, set sharply against it, the refrain comes in again : this time, I fancy, with a sort of compressed bitterness at the futility of war :

> Come build in the *empty* house of the stare.

I think there is a heavier stress on *empty* for this verse.

51

Then comes the conclusion of the matter. *We had fed the heart on fantasies.* If you wish to know exactly what that meant to Yeats at that stage you will have to read much more of his poetry, and some Irish history. But I am inclined to think it embodies a certain truth about *all* wars : the fierce blind nationalism that is fed on dreams. *The heart's grown brutal from the fare :* that Irish war saw many cruel things on both sides, brutalities which seem inseparable from all such conflicts. In the next two lines he has dropped the ' *is* ' : *there is more substance in our enmities than in our love.* That again is true ; it is at the root of all wars and violence, because it is so much easier and quicker to give way to hatred than to tend and nourish love. In another poem Yeats put the same thought in a slightly different form :

> Things fall apart ; the centre cannot hold ;
> Mere anarchy is loosed upon the world. . . .
> The best lack all conviction, while the worst
> Are full of passionate intensity.[1]

And then the refrain comes in with a new tone, returning in part to the invocation of the first line. Now it is a plea for regeneration by wisdom ; the stare's nest is the body (for the bird is a soul-symbol) and he prays that wisdom may enter into it :

> O honey-bees,
> Come build in the empty house of the stare.

2

And now I want to digress for a moment. It is just possible that some of you may have seen, or read of, the practice of an older generation in extracting from the works of poets a series of Great Thoughts, and serving them on different-coloured dishes to the reading public. The dish might be in one of several

---

[1] *The Second Coming.*

shapes : tear-off daily calendars, little suède-bound books for my lady's chamber, even shaving-blocks with tear-off papers, for when you used the ' cut-throat' razor you wiped the blade with a piece of shaving-paper. (No bad thing, this last custom ; for some reason that I do not understand, the mind is specially attentive and receptive when shaving.) Now all this seems slightly ridiculous to us ; and it is obviously bad that a middle section of the reading public should think a great writer to consist of nothing but rich quotational plums. At the same time there is one thing worth noting : the great *sententiæ*, important thoughts crystallized out into their perfect form, linger continually in the mind. They are apt, I think, to become *symbols* of the whole work ; and by recalling the symbol the reader can re-create at will something of the original response which he knew at the first reading. Furthermore, if literature is the record of the best and wisest things that men have thought, then it is clearly no bad thing for us to live with these memorable things. I do not suggest for one moment that you should consider them as a direct and explicit morality that is to be served up to you. The leaven of poetry works in many curious ways : and certainly many of these ways are in the subconscious. But through the ages they have worked thus on men's minds. ' Longinus ' put it in his own fashion, when he urged would-be writers to read and imitate the classics. " Here is my own mark, my friend, let us hold closely to it : for many are borne along inspired by a breath which comes from another, even as the story is that the Pythian prophetess " (that is, of the oracle at Delphi) " approaching the tripod, which is a cleft in the ground, inhales, so they say, the vapour sent by a god " (hence the origin of the word *inspiration*) ; " and then and there, impregnated by the divine power, sings her inspired chant ; even so from the great genius of men of old do streams pass off to the souls of those who emulate them, as though from holy caves. . . ."

At the other end of the scale read a schoolboy story by Kipling called *Regulus* : I will not spoil it for you by trying to give you the gist of it. And then think that your generation and mine are the first in the history of British thought since the Renaissance which have been cut off from the Greek and Roman Classics, and all that they implied. Finally, think of Matthew Arnold : " (The classical writers of antiquity) . . . can help to cure us of what is, it seems to me, the great vice of our intellect, manifesting itself in our incredible vagaries in literature, in art, in religion, in morals ; namely, that it is *fantastic*, and wants *sanity*. Sanity—that is the great virtue of the ancient literature : the want of that is the great defect of the modern, in spite of all its variety and power." [1] And then think on a fact within the experience of every tutor here : that, among undergraduates reading arts, it is long odds that the classic, or the man trained in classics, will be, by and large, ' better ' than his fellows. I use this word ' better ' with reluctance : but I mean by it moral qualities of balance and steadfastness, as well as a better-trained and more flexible mind.

3

The second poem is, at first glance, on a different plane. I have chosen it in order to suggest that you will find in poetry, from time to time, experiences that one receives with something of a healthy shock. Such, for example, were the first two poems we looked at, the ballad and Hardy's poem about the pet dog.

Now consider the thought of a girl making up. The face is smeared with ingredients which are, essentially, hogs' lard, oxide of iron, and sifted chalk or powdered rice. From the Bible onwards the painted face has been synonymous with falsehood, harlotry : you remember Hamlet's outburst against Ophelia and womanhood in general :

> I have heard of your paintings too, well enough ; God hath given you one face, and you make yourselves another : you jig, you amble, and you lisp, and nickname God's creatures, and make your wantonness your ignorance. [2]

---

[1] Preface to *Poems*, 1853.   [2] *Hamlet*, iii, 1.

And Hamlet again, to Yorick's skull :

> Now get you to my lady's chamber, and tell her, let her paint
> an inch thick, to this favour she shall come.[1]

Now listen to the poem on this girl :

> If I make the lashes dark
> And the eyes more bright
> And the lips more scarlet,
> Or ask if all be right
> From mirror after mirror,
> No vanity's displayed :
> I'm looking for the face I had
> Before the world was made.
>
> What if I look upon a man
> As though on my beloved,
> And my blood be cold the while
> And my heart unmoved ?
> Why should he think me cruel
> Or that he is betrayed ?
> I'd have him love the thing that was
> Before the world was made.

It is very simple, with the simplicity of high craftsmanship :
for through it Yeats has conveyed a kind of arrogance on the
part of the girl, pathetic in her search for the ideal beauty, the
ideal personality that time and circumstance have destroyed.
Each word in the poem is doing its full work :

> Or *ask* if all be *right*
> From mirror *after* mirror.

She *asks* from the mirrors, and there is a pathetic illusion there ;
she asks if all be *right*, whether the painting is perfect, and in
the repeated inspection, at different angles, in the mirrors ;
so that the word *after* gives, I think, the hint of meticulous and
yet wearisome care. The suppressed defiance, hinted at in the
first *If*—for she knows she will be blamed for it—breaks out in

---

[1] *Hamlet*, v, 1.

the next line, which rings out almost in isolation, triumphantly

> No vanity's displayed.

And then the dramatic justification, the accent falling on *had*:

> I'm looking for the face I had
> Before the world was made.

Her beauty, the ideal beauty, has been lost. She was meant to have it : and now, pitifully, she is trying to re-create it with lard, and iron rust, and mascara.

The thought is carried a stage further. She had been denied (perhaps ' in the corrupted currents of this world ') the beauty that was her due, and the love that was hers by right :

> What if I look upon a man
> As though on my beloved,
> And my blood be cold the while
> And my heart unmoved ?

By her pitiful acting, she is seeking to show her lover the personality that she has lost, just as she has lost her beauty. The nearest she can get to it is through this outward mask of love, of emotion she does not feel. What is the truth ? If we are denied beauty and love, is it best to take on the mask, to try to overcome circumstance ? Is life, perhaps, just such a conquest ? Maybe the beauty and love that she was meant to have will be recovered, in some measure, by the search for them.

4

These two poems, then, I have put before you to suggest how experiences within our normal range may be handled by a poet. In many, perhaps most instances, you have to go out, as it were, to meet the poem, as you had to with Donne and Blake ; and then having re-created it by sympathy and study you lead it back, as it were, to the circle of your own knowledge. But when it takes shape as an experience of which you can say " Ah, that is he " (or it), you will realize that the very formulation within the framework of the poem is in itself an activity that modifies the whole impact of the experience upon you, even though you believe yourself to be aware of it as " what oft was thought, but ne'er so well expressed ". Often the groundwork, the bare data, will appear familiar : but you will be hard put to it to formulate just what has happened within the poem. As an experiment, I am going to read aloud to you such a poem, and see what you make of it. It is the first of three poems called *Lessons of the War*, and the sub-title is *Naming of Parts*. At the head of it there is a quotation from Horace with one word altered—*duellis* instead of *puellis*—

Vixi duellis nuper idoneus
Et militavi non sine gloria

To-day we have naming of parts. Yesterday,
We had daily cleaning. And to-morrow morning,
We shall have what to do after firing. But to-day,
To-day we have naming of parts. Japonica
Glistens like coral in all of the neighbouring gardens,
    And to-day we have naming of parts.

This is the lower sling swivel. And this
Is the upper sling swivel, whose use you will see,
When you are given your slings. And this is the piling swivel,
Which in your case you have not got. The branches
Hold in the gardens their silent, eloquent gestures,
    Which in our case we have not got.

This is the safety-catch, which is always released
With an easy flick of the thumb. And please do not let me
See anyone using his finger. You can do it quite easy
If you have any strength in your thumb. The blossoms
Are fragile and motionless, never letting anyone see
    Any of them using their finger.

And this you can see is the bolt. The purpose of this
Is to open the breech, as you see. We can slide it
Rapidly backwards and forwards : we call this
Easing the spring. And rapidly backwards and forwards
The early bees are assaulting and fumbling the flowers :
    They call it easing the Spring.

They call it easing the Spring : it is perfectly easy
If you have any strength in your thumb : like the bolt,
And the breech, and the cocking-piece, and the point of balance,
Which in our case we have not got ; and the almond-blossom
Silent in all of the gardens and the bees going backwards and
    forwards,
    For to-day we have naming of parts.[1]

[1] Henry Reed, *A Map of Verona.*

CHAPTER VI

Two Passages from Shakespeare

I

THERE is no doubt in my mind, from what individual members of this audience have told me, that Shakespeare, for many of you, was largely spoilt in school; partly because of the pressure of examinations, and the often unenlightened drudgery of 'set books'; partly because few teachers manage to make Shakespeare 'live', and dissection is probably easier on the dead. They fail in this last, I think, because they tend to suggest to the schoolboy that the plays are museum pieces (understandable only with notes, and in essence and situation quite unrelated to modern thinking), and stress insufficiently what every great Shakespearian critic has noted—the psychological truth (even to the psychological inconsistencies) of Shakespeare's writing. No one who has served in a great headquarters in war can fail to be astounded at the accuracy of the picture of a General Staff given in *Troilus and Cressida*; some of you will know the living quality of certain of the issues presented, say, in *Measure for Measure*, or *A Winter's Tale*. (I give these as examples, because I hope you will start again on some of the lesser-known plays.) *King Lear* remains a living presentation of the central problems of the relationships between parents and children, problems which look like being accentuated by our present taxation, the social revolution, and the operations of the welfare state. You doubt that? Listen to Lear, denied by Regan, told by her to return to Goneril and beg his daughter's pardon:

Ask her forgiveness ?
Do you but mark how this becomes the house :
' Dear daughter, I confess that I am old ;
Age is unnecessary : on my knees I beg
That you'll vouchsafe me raiment, bed, and food.' [1]

Now, I do not suggest that all plays present so clearly a
' criticism of life '—' the powerful application of ideas to life ' :
but if you will go back to them with clear eyes, and with some
knowledge of the subtleties of this kind of verse as a vehicle
for thought you will find a new world of pleasure. All that I
can do this morning is to take two passages from plays that you
will know, and talk about them. In this I feel that I am rather
like the man who, offering a house for sale, carried in his pocket
a brick from it to show to intending purchasers. (But then that
criticism applies to all this course :

' Had we but world enough and time . . .')

2

I am going to take first a passage from *Macbeth*. You will
remember the context. Macbeth is alone. The servants have
just passed across the hall with the dishes from the feast now
being served to the guest and King whom he proposes to murder.
He has left the great chamber to collect his thoughts. All the
workings of his mind are against the murder. It would not
matter so greatly if the act could terminate with itself. But
there is judgment, even in this world, to follow. He owes a
double (or a triple) trust to Duncan : as kinsman and subject to
the King, and as his host. But there is another reason, and now
the verse swells and changes in key :

Besides, this Duncan
Hath borne his faculties so meek, hath been
So clear in his great office, that his virtues

---

[1] *King Lear*, ii, 4.

Will plead like angels, trumpet-tongu'd against
The deep damnation of his taking off;
And pity, like a naked new-born babe,
Striding the blast, or heaven's cherubin, hors'd
Upon the sightless couriers of the air,
Shall blow the horrid deed in every eye,
That tears shall drown the wind. I have no spur
To prick the sides of my intent, but only
Vaulting ambition, which o'er-leaps itself
And falls on the other.

[*Enter* LADY MACBETH [1]

Consider first this strange language : where every word seems
to fall or grow into place. This is the mark of great writing.
And yet the words are a little strange. Duncan

Hath borne his faculties so meek, hath been
So *clear* in his great office . . .

The virtues are modesty and incorruptibility: *clear*, which means
eminent, distinguished; and perhaps the image of water or fire,
clear as contrasted with the muddied soul of the politician, the
intriguer. And these are, perhaps, among the soldier's virtues,
the virtues for which Macbeth himself has won his reputation ;
for which he has just been promoted. These virtues will *plead
like angels*—messengers of God—against the crime. But *plead* is
in sharp contrast to *trumpet-tongu'd*. Now the trumpeter in the
law court who announces the coming of the Judge, does not
plead. What has been achieved is, I think, one of those incredible
images—perhaps based on a picture, of angels blowing their

---

[1] The whole passage is a remarkable illustration of the way in which personal
considerations may intrude themselves. To a certain Bomber Pilot the whole
imagery suggested the air and aircraft. *So clear in his great office* suggested the pilot,
encased in Perspex: *the office* being slang for the cockpit. *Angels* suggested,
phonetically, *engines*, and the *trumpets* the roar of them preparatory to taking-off.
Further, the codeword for ' thousands of feet ', in height, was *angels* ; ten
angels=10,000 feet. *Taking off* needs no explanation. *Striding the blast* referred
to the aircraft over the target, with the bomb-doors open ; the *sightless couriers*
a squadron flying at a great height in cloud. For him, the whole passage was
linked to the pity and terror of night operations.

trumpets (many poets draw imagery from painting)—which
are composed, as it were, of a double over-lay—*plead* and
trumpet-tongu'd—gentleness, conviction, majesty and judgment ;
all as it were fused in the line.

Then follows the most astonishing image :

> And pity, like a naked new-born babe,
> Striding the blast, . . .

Now Blake illustrated this, but saw in it something very
different, I think, from Shakespeare's thought. Yet I will
describe Blake's drawing to you, since I believe that there is a
strong visual basis in Macbeth's lyrical and horrified contemplation of the possible consequences of his act. In Blake's engraving
a woman is lying upon the ground, as in death, for her garments
are as if sculptured in stone, and like grave-clothes. Above
her, springing upwards, is an infant form, radiant with light,
giving the impression of being a kind of miniature man, fully
developed, rather than an infant. Above are two white horses,
blind, thrust out in long flowing line that harmonizes with a
background of storm, of daimonic cosmic energy. The riders
of the horses are women, with flowing hair ; the nearer of the
two is leaning over her horse's flank, with a look of infinite pity,
to catch up to her the babe that is leaping upwards from its
dead mother.

Go back to those lines again

> And pity, like a naked new-born babe,
> Striding the blast . . .

Pity as a naked defenceless babe—yes : but—*striding the blast* ?
At once there is a double image forming—*striding* for power,
mastery over the elements, denying the weakness of the babe,
adding to the elemental mystery of the thing called pity :
just as the angels pleaded *trumpet-tongu'd*. But the babe is also,
prophetically, the emblem of revenge upon the murderer ;
the second and third Apparitions in the Cavern with the witches,
the Bloody Child and the Child Crowned. And the angels are

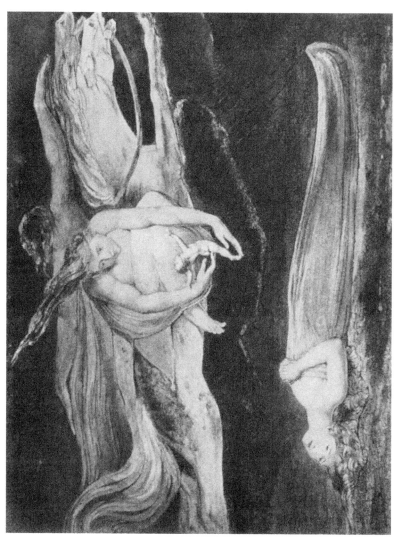

BLAKE: *Pity*

still in the complex fabric of the background, so that the picture shifts its shape :

> or heaven's cherubin, hors'd
> Upon the sightless couriers of the air . . .

We spoke before of the horse as an archetypal image : remember Marvell's *wingèd chariot*. The blind [1] choosers of the slain, the wild horses that thunder across the sky in Ibsen's *Rosmersholm*, seem to be kin to these. The thought rising steadily in Macbeth's mind is now of fear : fear of judgment with strong angels pleading against the murder, fear of the terrible blind horses in the sky, of the storm that his evil will bring about.

> . . . Shall blow the horrid deed in every eye
> That tears shall drown the wind . . .

Now his thought returns, as it were, on the rim of the circle : *pity—tears—wind*, the blast that pity strides, calmed by tears. Yet it is all so complex that neither you nor I dare to put it into words.

Then he swings back to consider himself, the agent of the murder :

> I have no spur

(the horse image, with the launching of cosmic forces in the storm, is still in his mind)

> To prick the sides of my intent, but only
> Vaulting ambition,

By all counts, we are getting near a mixed metaphor : we must make a heavy sense-break after *intent*. *I have only . . . vaulting ambition* : ambition from a sudden upward impetus, the spur ; ambition (now identified with the rider) that fails to hold his seat in the saddle. (This is just what is going to happen ; and the horse is to return in another form : for when he says

> I did hear
> The galloping of horse. Who was't came by ?

---

[1] It may be that the cherubin are to be thought of as clear-sighted—cf. ' the young-ey'd cherubins '—in contrast with the horses.

it is Macduff escaping to raise the armies of justice against the regicide and usurper.) And *the sightless couriers* ? The witches have just ridden off—

> Infected be the air whereon they *ride*,
> And damn'd all those that trust them . . .

Make what you like of these echoes and cross-references to the terror of the horse ; only know that they are there for the finding. Shakespeare is full of them. Now go back and read that passage again, and feel all that is in it beyond speech or understanding.

2

King Lear, v, 3

> No, no, no, no ! Come, let's away to prison ;
> We two alone will sing like birds i' the cage :
> When thou dost ask me blessing, I'll kneel down,
> And ask of thee forgiveness : so we'll live,
> And pray, and sing, and tell old tales, and laugh
> At gilded butterflies, and hear poor rogues
> Talk of court news ; and we'll talk with them too,
> Who loses and who wins ; who's in, who's out ;
> And take upon's the mystery of things,
> As if we were God's spies : and we'll wear out,
> In a wall'd prison, packs and sets of great ones
> That ebb and flow by the moon.

I have taken for my second example this speech from *Lear*. At the last moment, apparently on the edge of freedom, Lear and Cordelia have been captured by Edmund's forces. Edmund orders them to be led away to await ' censure ' from the two sisters. Cordelia asks whether they are not to confront ' these daughters and these sisters '. This is Lear's reply.

For me this passage contains the distilled essence of much

of *Lear*. The King has passed through his suffering on the heath. He has been reconciled to Cordelia and found peace in her arms. He is still in part mad, but is seeing many things clearly, and in peace, even in a strange exaltation. All the petulance and the ravings have died out of the rhythms of his speech ; and instead you have this lyric utterance. Into these lines, in the aftermath of madness, are caught up many of the threads that make the conflict of the play : scene after scene is echoed in it. The King rejoices in the prospect of prison, since they two are alone. They will *sing like birds i' the cage* : remember how the whole of the rest of *Lear* is shot through and through with imagery taken from beasts and reptiles—serpents, lions, wolves, bears, as man goes back to beast against a background of storm, till he is stript naked. But now it is the bird : the ethereal thing, the symbol of the soul. They are to be birds, singing even in the cage. The scene where he rejected Cordelia, refused her blessing (and then cursed Goneril with the terrible curse of sterility) is now reversed.

> so we'll *live*

(A few lines after the end of the speech Edmund gives an officer orders that they are to be killed in prison.)

> —And pray, and sing, and tell old tales, and laugh
> At gilded butterflies—

Is a butterfly gilded ? But Shakespeare is thinking as a madman, and the butterfly is the courtier, in the language of the time, with his wealth, his *gilding*, his fine dress, and his inanities. That is why his thoughts turn, in the next line, to politics and the court

> —and hear poor rogues
> Talk of court news ; and we'll talk with them too
> Who loses and who wins ; who's in, who's out.

(Remember, they are themselves the victims of battles suddenly lost and won ; politics and war, both are at the mercy of fortune.

65

And the play opens with a great court scene, staged to satisfy Lear's arrogance and pride of power.)

Then there come—just as the Macbeth speech swelled up to its lyric climax—the miraculous lines :

> And take upon's the mystery of things
> As if we were God's spies . . .

Again we are dealing with thought beyond that which we can draw immediately from the words. As for the word *spies*, its evil sense has been killed, as it were, by what precedes it, and we are back to the old meaning of the observer, he who gathers information, that he may report his knowledge to God. To take upon oneself—old, mad, and in prison, the mystery of life : to accept it gladly and joyfully—all this is implicit in the statement.

> and we'll wear out
> In a wall'd prison, packs and sets of great ones
> That ebb and flow by the moon.

Again the paradox of their security in prison ; the utter acceptance of life to which madness has brought the King, even while his death is being prepared. *Packs* and *sets*—the hard consonants and the crisp vowels are suggestive of contempt for court and politics—again—a theme of the whole play—even if it were not for the suggestion of the wolf-pack and the cabal, lending irony to the *great ones*. They *ebb and flow by the moon* ; at the mercy of the cycles of fortune (as his own fortunes have swayed) : the moon being the familiar symbol—inconstancy, mistress of the tides that rule the affairs of men. Look, when you re-read the plays, for the moon-tide image, in all its complexities and shades of meaning. And think that there is (as here) something mysterious in the cadence of the last line, even to the rhythm checked by the extra syllable, *by the moon* : and set beside it the impact of Donne's

> dull *sublunary* lovers' love

and Cleopatra on the death of Antony :

> O wither'd is the garland of the war,
> The soldier's pole is fall'n ; young boys and girls
> Are level now with men ; the odds is gone,
> And there is nothing left remarkable
> Beneath the visiting moon.[1]

and Hamlet to the Ghost :

> What may this mean,
> That thou, dead corse, again in complete steel
> Revisit'st thus the glimpses of the moon. . . .[2]

3

Now I do not for an instant suggest that all Shakespearian poetry is as rich dramatically, or as complex in language, as these two passages. What I am suggesting is that here is a mine to work whose riches you will never exhaust. Go to the plays again as human documents, studies of living types, with poetry that contains within itself not only this wealth of meaning in language, but which is in addition shot through and through with the added richness of dramatic irony, allusion, counter-pointed themes and harmonies, and half-determined symbols that ' set the mind wandering from idea to idea, from emotion to emotion '. Go, in this new start of yours, to some of the plays you will not have read at school : *A Winter's Tale, Troilus and Cressida, Measure for Measure*. Read *Love's Labour's Lost* for what it is : a most brilliant, light-hearted, topical revue, topical by reason of its allusions to contemporary personalities, fads, cliques, of the society of the day. Then go back to the great tragedies, thinking of them from two main points of view ; first, as plays dealing with basic psychological types, permanent and modern under their Elizabethan dress.

---

[1] *Antony and Cleopatra*, iv, 15.   [2] *Hamlet*, i, 4.

Secondly, consider how the great artist can make, out of evil, misery, frustration, something that is aesthetically and morally satisfying, and opens up a glimpse, at the last, of what we may call ' reality ', though no one can define just what he understands by the word in the context.

And the strange thing about it is this sense of exaltation. Yeats has put it better than I can.

> All perform their tragic play,
> There struts Hamlet, there is Lear,
> That's Ophelia, that Cordelia ;
> Yet they, should the last scene be there,
> The great stage curtain about to drop,
> If worthy their prominent part in the play
> Do not break up their lines to weep.
> They know that Hamlet and Lear are gay ;
> Gaiety transfiguring all that dread.
> All men have aimed at, found and lost ;
> Black out ; heaven blazing into the head :
> Tragedy wrought to its uttermost.[1]

We know little about the real nature of tragedy. It is like some highly complex element, the components of which we can analyse up to a certain point ; but we do not and cannot know just how its restless particles react upon each other, and upon us, in the complex organism of a play.

[1] *Lapis Lazuli.*

68

Two Passages from the Bible :
Ecclesiastes XI, 9–10, and XII
and Matthew VI, 19–34

I

I MAKE no apology for drawing your attention to the poetry of the Bible, and its importance in your lives and mine. Our everyday speech is shot through and through with its idiom and its imagery : whether we admit it or not, our way of thought has been conditioned by it, in greater or less measure, for perhaps a thousand years. Its very rhythms and its cadences are akin to the phrases we use.

How long this will continue I do not know. It is certain that our ears are growing steadily less accustomed to hearing the Bible read aloud ; but, at a guess, we are unlikely to forget it for a good many years yet. We dare not forget it if we are going to understand English poetry.

I am going to try to lay aside all theological issues, and to invite your attention to some of the poetry of the Bible, and to suggest, perhaps, how it should be read ; bringing to your notice certain characteristics that may make the Bible a greater delight to hear or read. Remember first how the Authorized Version came into being. It was the work of forty-seven translators, going back to Hebrew and Greek, but with earlier English Versions in front of them ; intending to make the best possible synthesis out of these early versions : filing and fitting language in the certainty that they could undertake no greater work than to render, with all possible dignity and weight, the

meaning of the original (as far as they could) so that it should be
' understanded of the people '. I used the words *filed* and *fitted* ;
for if you look at those earlier versions you will see them at
work on very much the same process as a poet uses as he revises
draft after draft ; till he has before him (though he is never
satisfied) " the best words in the best order ". Just what that
phrase means we shall see later from a comparison of some of the
versions.

Hebrew was the simple language of a people whose daily
concern was with simple things : corn and wine and oil ;
rivers and flocks ; using the warfare images of a small people
living uneasily with their neighbours—the chariot and horses,
the bow, the arrow that flieth by day. They were fighting for
the supremacy of their God, Jehovah, among a horde of
picturesque idolators, whose fish-gods and brazen images were
a perpetual temptation to error. In the midst of a tumultuous
history of wars, captivities, exiles, and oppressions, they clung,
with the same inner pertinacity that marks the race to-day, to
their concern with ultimate values ; the meaning of the universe,
the ways of God to man, and of man to God. The moods
recorded in their literature vary from the tenderness and
exaltation of love to the most savage brutality and treachery :
from records of supreme nobility to those of almost every
imaginable crime : through epic, myth, fantasy, love poetry,
invective, prophecy, bardic genealogies, catalogues of buildings
and temple furnishings, and distilled collections of the proverbial
wisdom of the eastern Mediterranean. The Hebrew language
was well suited for translation into the English of the early
seventeenth century : both were simple, direct, vivid, perpetually
concerned with things seen and felt ; and (because lacking in
abstract terms) constrained to approach thoughts too great and
complex, either through language of the utmost simplicity
(" Let there be light ") or through myth, or parable, or paradox.
There was ready for it an English tradition which had attained
great strength of sinewy prose in the Elizabethan Voyagers ;

which had already built up a vehicle of rhetoric in the sermon, and which was about to absorb from Greek and Latin the new scientific and abstract vocabulary which was necessary to express its new apprehensions. Its great potential failing, the tendency to fall into long and confused sentences through too close a following of the inflected Latin, was avoided completely by the short, incisive, Hebrew constructions.

When you read, remember two things : Hebrew poetry depends upon *parallelism*, saying the same, or nearly the same thing, twice, usually in the same verse, or repeating, with a slight change, or enlargement, the first thought. Secondly, remember their scheme of references, their surroundings, their preoccupations, the impact of their daily life upon their expressions ; and try to think (as we thought of the rose-image) of their language as fresh and vivid again, not as something staled by repetition, or only half-realized by reason of its very familiarity.

I am now going to read a passage from the end of Ecclesiastes. I have chosen it because the writer (if indeed it is the work of one writer only) seems to have been a man whose temper is, in some ways, not unlike that of many of us to-day. He has not entirely accepted the divine revelation. He is struggling to discover the meaning of life ; he has only partially succeeded. He is bewildered and pessimistic : but here at the end of the book he is lifted up into a kind of noble stoicism, lit at the last by a gleam of acceptance. I am going to read it, and comment, and suggest parallels as I do so.

> Rejoice, O young man, in thy youth, and let thy heart cheer thee in the days of thy youth, and walk in the ways of thine heart, and in the sight of thine eyes ; but know thou, that for all these things God will bring thee into judgment. Therefore remove sorrow from thy heart, and put away evil from thy flesh : for childhood and youth are vanity.

Now, immediately, you have a seeming paradox, arising from

the first and the last sentence. *Rejoice in thy youth.* That is good and wise advice : provided that cheer comes from the *heart*, that is, from the inner and unified being, in psychological harmony. We are to obey our inner conscience and to see things clearly and objectively. But there will be judgment ; which, even if we lay aside theology, we can interpret as a warning of the inexorable law that whatever evil we commit we pay for. At the same time we are told to remove *sorrow* from our heart—useless repining for the past or future; Yeats was right, in this sense, when he wrote:

> Repentance keeps my heart impure . . .

Vanity gives the wrong sense (in our usage) unless we can go back to its source : for here it means literally *breath* or *vapour*, that which is illusory, either by reason of its unstable form, or because it is of the fleeting nature of mere speech.

That is perhaps true. How many of us would go through our schooldays again—in spite of all the pompous pronouncements at Speech Days ? So Yeats again :

> . . . Endure that toil of growing up ;
> The ignominy of boyhood ; the distress
> Of boyhood changing into man ;
> The unfinished man and his pain
> Brought face to face with his own clumsiness . . . [1]

Now comes the familiar passage :

> Remember now thy Creator in the days of thy youth, while the evil days come not, nor the years draw nigh, when thou shalt say, I have no pleasure in them ; while the sun, or the light, or the moon, or the stars, be not darkened, nor the clouds return after the rain.

You and I will pass into old age, and its querulous decrepitude,

[1] *A Dialogue of Self and Soul.*

and maybe see the decay, or the end, of civilization. That knowledge is valuable to sharpen our sense of living, the employment of the 'delighted senses' in the present. Then, very simply, the writer builds up his picture of a desolate, empty universe, cold and unliving ; when to an old person or to an outworn civilization, all the natural processes are arrested, silent : *nor the clouds return after the rain* ; where that exquisite cadence suggests the recurrent sorrows of an old man, as he feels his powers ebbing. (*Cloud—sorrow* is a standard comparison.) Then, in a succession of homely images, he drives home the idea of a deserted arid life ; as an old man might see it, looking out from a ruin in a deserted village in Palestine.

> In the day when the keepers of the house shall tremble, and the strong men shall bow themselves, and the grinders cease because they are few, and those that look out of the windows be darkened, and the doors shall be shut in the streets, when the sound of the grinding is low, and he shall rise up at the voice of the bird, and all the daughters of music shall be brought low.

The majority of commentators agree in interpreting the *keepers of the house* as the hands and arms ; *the strong men* as the knees, tottering in old age ; the *grinders* as the teeth ; *those that look out of the windows* as the eyes ; the *doors . . . in the streets* as the lips. But these interpretations are, I think, secondary to the poetic impression. The picture of decay and desolation is undoubted : and I have an image of the sentries and the soldiers deserting, and the sound of the corn-mills ceasing as the village falls into decay. In the next sentence the intention is, it is said, to convey the increasing deafness of the old—the sound of bird song grows faint, and all the notes of human song sink low. But surely the picture is also of a House of Death : where all life is ebbing, and the hired mourners are waiting on the threshold to begin their lamentation.

Beyond and *through* the meaning, you can hear how the

rhythm sways and changes to convey the subtlety of emotion :
the rising scale of

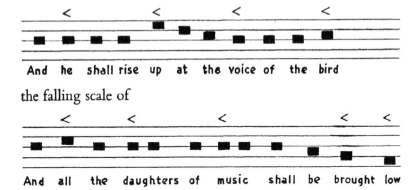

the falling scale of

Then he builds up again. Some of you will remember
Campion's description, which he took from Horace, of the
virtuous man :

> He only can behold
> With unaffrighted eyes
> The horrors of the deep
> And terrors of the skies.

Here, then, are the 'terrors of the skies':

> Also when they shall be afraid of that which is high, and fears
> shall be in the way, and the almond tree shall flourish, and the
> grasshopper shall be a burden, and desire shall fail . . .

That which is high : the ambiguity that can denote storm, or the
justice of God, or (as some interpret prophecies) the modern
'terror of the skies'. (It is not altogether an idle fancy to see
prophecies fulfilled in poetry ; it does at least sharpen our
awareness of them. Make what you like of Bishop King's

> And a fierce Feaver must calcine
> The body of the world like thine.[1])

Or—for Hebrew Poetry is apt to carry these ambiguities—it

[1] *The Exequy.*

74

may be still no more than a picture of old age, fearful of climbing steep places, or of accidents in the traffic of the streets. All great writers write better than they know. *Fears in the way*—wolves or bandits on the roads ; the almond tree that flourishes among ruins ; the plague of insects that brings famine. See how the prose moves, as it were, in an arc, as the writer's thoughts move from sky to roads, and then the fields about the village ; then with famine comes the withering of man's virility, the negation of life,

> . . . because man goeth to his long home, and the mourners go about the streets.

The mourners are the hired wailers who go perpetually from one funeral to another. I do not think it is fantastic to see—an Elizabethan would have seen it—the ambiguity in the phrase ' his long home ' ; remember Shakespeare :

> Fare thee well, great heart !
> Ill-weav'd ambition, how much art thou shrunk !
> When that this body did contain a spirit,
> A kingdom for it was too great a bound ;
> But now two paces of the vilest earth
> Is room enough.[1]

Now we are in the midst of image and symbol :

> Or ever the silver cord be loosed, or the golden bowl be broken, or the pitcher be broken at the fountain, or the wheel broken at the cistern.

It is thought that the *silver cord* and the *golden bowl* refer to the hanging lamp in the temple. But they are symbols ' in depth ' : *Cord*—thread—the thread of life, the three Fates—Milton's

> . . . Comes the blind Fury with th' abhorrèd shears,
> And slits the thin spun life . . .

all are aspects of the symbol. Some interpret the loosening of the silver cord to be the silencing of the tongue, or the breaking

[1] *I Henry IV*, v, 4.

of the spinal cord, in death ; but this seems improbable. So, too, for the *golden bowl* : " golden " in the Bible (and in the Scottish Ballads) is the symbol of a primitive people for all that is most precious, rare, indestructible. The bowl is that which contains *oil*, a life symbol everywhere : as giving fire, so that lamp, wick, and oil bear complex meanings of eternity, resurrection, sexual potency.

(Think of Shelley's

> When the lamp is shattered
> The light in the dust lies dead.)

So the pitcher, made of clay, dust ; in the form of the womb ; the container of the water, so precious to a Mediterranean people ; the body containing the soul ; the body broken at length by its arduous service. Linked to the pitcher is the wheel of the cistern, the bringer of fertility which, when it breaks, lets the whole machinery fall into the cistern : fountain, cistern, pitcher, wheel, broken and collapsed in death. " Then "—and all that has gone before has been a great organ-like prelude to convey this sense of resignation. The worst has been faced ; the conflict is resolved :

> Then shall the dust return to the earth as it was, and the spirit
> shall return unto God who gave it.

The pitcher is ground again into the clay : spirit—wind or water, the mysterious and unpredictable things—return to their sources.

> Vanity of vanities, saith the Preacher, all is vanity.

The sense of *vanity* is given more accurately when we know that an alternative translation for *vanity* is *vapour*. Think of Antony, confronting his ruin, pondering on the unsubstantial nature of reality :

> Sometimes we see a cloud that's dragonish ;
> A vapour sometime like a bear or lion,
> A tower'd citadel, a pendant rock,

A forked mountain, or blue promontory
With trees upon't, that nod unto the world
And mock our eyes with air : thou hast seen these signs ;
They are black vesper's pageants.
EROS.   Ay, my lord.
ANTONY. That which is now a horse, even with a thought
The rack dislimns, and makes it indistinct,
As water is in water.[1]

But the poem does not end there. We drop for a moment, deliberately :

> And, moreover, because the Preacher was wise, he still taught the people knowledge ; yea, he gave good heed, and sought out, and set in order, many proverbs. The Preacher sought to find acceptable words, and that which was written was upright, even words of truth. The words of the wise are as goads, and as nails fastened by the masters of assemblies, which are given from one shepherd.

A curious, homely pair of images : *goads* driving them on to work, or to war, or to virtue : *nails* (one thinks of Luther and his proclamation), the defiant or authoritative proclamation of a truth. And here I quote from John Stuart Mill's *System of Logic*. " Hardly any original thoughts on mental or social subjects ever make their way among mankind, or assume their proper importance in the minds even of their inventors, until aptly selected words and phrases have, as it were, *nailed them down and held them fast*." The words of the wise are half-personified, bound together in collections. *Goad* and *shepherd* go naturally together, image of a pastoral people. He goes on :

> And further, by these, my son, be admonished : of making many books there is no end, and much study is a weariness of the flesh.

You can think of that in all its meanings, but especially (to make it fresh in your minds) think of it as the outcry of a

[1] *Antony and Cleopatra*, iv, 12.

77

disillusioned and tired man, writing in the tradition of the East, of this seemingly unending mass of traditional ' wisdom ', proverb lore, dark and esoteric utterances ; the tradition of infinite verbal memorizing, the same tradition that was to bring forth the proverbial sterility, the ' letter of the law '.

And then a passage on which it would be presumptuous to comment :

> Let us hear the conclusion of the whole matter : Fear God, and keep his commandments : for this is the whole duty of man. For God shall bring every work into judgment, with every secret thing, whether it be good, or whether it be evil.

2

I referred just now to the filing and fitting of language, till it becomes (in poetry) " the best words in the best order ". The passage you have before you was worked at Cambridge by the two groups of translators here. Two others worked at Oxford, and two at Westminster. Here are two of the earlier texts, set side by side with that of 1611 in its contemporary spelling. The first is from the Great Bible of 1539–40 (i) : the second from the Geneva Bible of 1560 (ii). Remember that the authors were not out to create a new translation, but to make the best possible synthesis of the previous translators, ' to find acceptable words '. You can see the process here.

A. (i) When the dores in the stretes shalbe shutt,
   (ii) And the dores shal be shut without
       And the doores shall be shut in the streets,

B. (i) and when the voyce of the myller shalbe layed
      downe :
   (ii) by the base sound of the grinding,
      when the sound of the grinding is low,

C. (i) when men shall ryse up at the voyce of the byrde,
   (ii) and he shall rise up at the voice of the birde :
        and he shall rise up at the voice of the bird,

D. (i) and when all the daughters of musike shalbe brought lowe :
   (ii) and all the daughters of singing shalbe abased.
        and all the daughters of musicke shall be brought low.

E. (i) when men shall feare in hye places, and be afrayed in the stretes :
   (ii) Also thei shalbe afraied of the hie thing, and feare shalbe in the way,
        also when they shalbe afraid of that which is high, and feares shall be in the way.

F. (i) when the Almonde tree shall florysh and be laden with the greshoper,
   (ii) and the almonde tre shal florish and the grashopper shalbe a burden,
        and the Almond tree shall flourish, and the grashopper shall be a burden.

G. (i) and when all lust shall passe
   (ii) and concupiscence shalbe driven away :
        and desire shall faile :

H. (i) (because when man goeth to hys longe home,
   (ii) for man goeth to the house of his age,
        because man goeth to his long home.

I. (i) and the mourners go aboute the stretes)
   (ii) and the mourners go about in the strete.
        and the mourners goe about the streets.

Now it is always a matter of difficulty to decide whether we are being entirely honest in establishing a preference for one version over another when the final one has become so familiar to us. But you can see the selection of the vigorous phrase, the shedding of the superfluous, and above all, the reorganization of language to produce a strong and noble rhythm in the beat of the verses. For example, the translators evidently thought that the Geneva Bible's

> Also thei shalbe afraied of the hie thing

was nearer to the Hebrew than Coverdale's

> Also they shall be afraid in hye places

but that compression and rhythm would be better served (and, I think, the sense of terror heightened by its very indeterminacy) in the rendering

> Also when they shall be afraid of that which is high.

In the same way, consider the simplicity of

> And desire shall faile

compared with

> And concupiscence shall be driven away

As for this last sentence, it is, I think, an instance of two things : the expansion of the thought far beyond that of the second version, and the reinforcement of the meaning by the rhythm.

> And desire shall faile

For the final version, though it includes *concupiscence*, is suddenly extended in its layers of meaning to all the desires of man's heart : and I think that we are meant to be aware of these 'layered' meanings of *desire* and *fail*, even to the sharpened 'i' of *desire* and the falling close of *fail*, growing faint and fainter on the liquid *l*.

3

The Greek of the New Testament is not a scholar's language, but that of a whole Mediterranean culture. These books as we have them were written eighty, a hundred and fifty, two hundred years after the death of the Founder. They represent men's recollections, traditions, of His words and teaching in the Aramaic which He used. Their language is the language of the countryside, of village life, of seed-time and harvest, ships and fishing ; robbers and tax-gatherers ; its parables and imagery drawn from such a life. But it could carry a greater range than the Hebrew, since the Greeks had forged it into an instrument for philosophy. It could deal with narrative in the Acts, 'phantasy' in Revelation, profound argument in Corinthians, with equal ease. As with the Old Testament, the genius of the language, and the certainty in the translators as to their high task, produced English that is sinewy, economical, shaped with the most exquisite taste.

My object is to discuss with you these instrumental qualities of language, and not matters of religion or theology. I have therefore chosen for you a familiar passage, containing proverbial phrases that have passed into our speech : yet which we accept without considering their meaning or their context. It is poetic language, rhetorical in the best sense of that much abused term : for rhetoric is the art of persuasion, and a great preacher or politician must persuade, using the language, the images, of everyday speech.

> Lay up for yourselves treasure in heaven, where neither moth nor rust doth corrupt, and where thieves do not break through nor steal . . .

(Cloth, weapons or iron ornaments, and gold and silver ; the things, I take it, subject to these three kinds of loss.)

> . . . For where your treasure is, there will your heart be also. The light of the body is the eye : if therefore thine eye be single, thy whole body shall be full of light. But if thine eye be evil, thy whole body shall be full of darkness. If therefore the light that is in thee be darkness, how great is that darkness !

A platitude, perhaps ; an image highly unscientific ; but at the root a *poetic* expression of a highly complex thought. ' A division of interest leads to a dispersion of personality.' (How ridiculous that sounds !) What *does* it mean, anyway ? " An obsession with material possessions obscures all spiritual values ? " Or is it that the man to whom has been given the gift of mental vision suffers, if he denies it, a far more profound disintegration than the man whose vision is only partial ? The eye—light-darkness image, with all its untidy edges, means far more than this : because light and darkness are perennial symbols, in all religions. And then we have to read the passage again with some knowledge of Jewish idiom : in which a *good eye* is a metaphor for liberality, and *evil eye* for one who is *grudging* in his gifts : so that the meaning of the passage is " If you are miserly and grudging, keeping your wealth for yourself, then spiritual light cannot penetrate into you ; and such light as you have becomes ever darker, till it ceases to be light, and becomes darkness." Thus it is connected, perfectly logically, with what went before and with what follows :

> Ye cannot serve God and Mammon. Therefore I say unto you, Take no thought for your life, what ye shall eat, or what ye shall drink, nor yet for your body, what ye shall put on. Is not the life more than meat, and the body than raiment ? Behold the fowls of the air : for they sow not, neither do they reap, nor gather into barns : yet your heavenly Father feedeth them. Are ye not much better than they ? Which of you by taking thought can add one cubit unto his stature ? And why take ye thought for raiment ? Consider the lilies of the field, how they grow : they toil not, neither do they spin ; and yet I say unto you that even Solomon in all his glory was not arrayed like one of these.

Instinctively you and I start to criticize it. The arguments are irrelevant. We no longer believe in a providence that feeds and clothes us. The state takes charge of our bodies, living and dead. The appeal to fowls and flowers is picturesque ; but we have seen birds dying by myriads in a hard winter, and the fields burned with drought. And the glory of a picturesque chief of a tiny eastern state twenty-nine centuries ago means little to us.

All right. Look at it again. Behind the picturesque language, the exaggeration, the colourful images, there is this truth, which is being driven home throughout this paragraph, *that obsession with the planning and actions of physical life obscures and distorts spiritual values, including personality itself.*

It is not written that we should renounce all effort and foresight and prudence, and live on our fellows : it is simply a poetic statement of that truth that undue reliance on planning is against the currents of the world ; that events as they emerge out of time are never such that we can impose our pattern upon them.

The passage from St. Matthew continues :

> Wherefore, if God so clothe the grass of the field, which to-day is, and to-morrow is cast into the oven, shall he not much more clothe you, O ye of little faith ? Therefore take no thought saying, What shall we eat ? or, What shall we drink ? or, Wherewithal shall we be clothed ? (for after all these things do the Gentiles seek :) for your heavenly Father knoweth that ye have need of all these things. . . . Take therefore no thought for the morrow : for the morrow shall take thought for the things of itself. Sufficient unto the day is the evil thereof.

I do not (I repeat) see in this an injunction to carelessness or improvidence ; but wise advice, proved time and again in the history of individuals and nations. Most of us eat out our hearts in attempting to provide against every possible contingency, in anticipating the difficulties that never come, in living in the past or future, and in the phantasies that they involve.

But apart from the wisdom of this poetry, consider the exquisite clarity and precision of language here ; the range of tone, the rhetorical questions, the incisive cutting edge of the short sentences, the use of scorn. So, too, the logical structure of the whole of this passage ; we can summarize the dominant themes, and see the expansion of thought round each, till the whole is finally locked together. Diagramatically the thoughts might be shown thus :

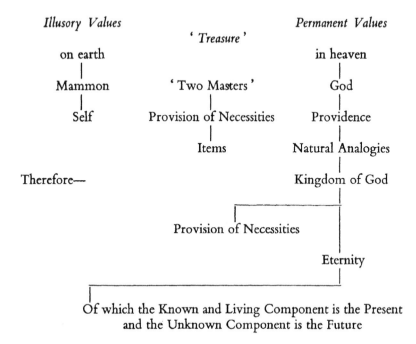

Illusory Values   Permanent Values
                    ' Treasure '
    on earth   in heaven
       | |
    Mammon   ' Two Masters '   God
       | |
    Self   Provision of Necessities Providence
                            | |
                          Items   Natural Analogies
                                              |
Therefore—   Kingdom of God
                                              |
                    Provision of Necessities
                                              |
                                          Eternity
                                              |

Of which the Known and Living Component is the Present
and the Unknown Component is the Future

You can read this kind of writing again and again, and learn to admire the economy and vividness of writing : the ' happy valiancy of phrases ' which is not a rhetorical device but the outcome of things apprehended with clear sight and with the emotion that is appropriate to them. Consider the descriptions in the parable of the Prodigal Son, or of the Good Samaritan in all their economy and insight into man's mind. Look at the realism of the descriptions of the sea, as in the terse accuracy of this :

> But when the fourteenth night was come, as we were driven up and down in Adria, about midnight the shipmen deemed that they drew near to some country ; and sounded, and found it twenty fathoms : and when they had gone a little further, they

sounded again, and found it fifteen fathoms. Then fearing lest we should have fallen upon rocks, they cast four anchors out of the stern, and wished for the day.[1]

The language is that of men who knew the sea ; down to the last superb detail of ' fallen *upon* rocks ', for the lift and scend of the waves on a drifting boat.

And here, for comparison, is a passage from an account of a voyage to Virginia, written in 1607, four years before the Authorized Version was published.

> When it grew to be towards night, we stood backe to our Ships, we sounded and found it shallow water for a great way, which put vs out of all hopes for getting any higher with our Ships, which road at the Mouth of the Riuer. Wee rowed ouer to a point of Land, where wee found a channell ; and sounded six, eight, ten, or twelve fathom : which put us in good comfort. Therefore wee named that point of Land, Cape *Comfort*.[2]

4

Now I am not suggesting that you should take the Bible as a model for your English prose. Many great writers have done so, but it seems unlikely that it can be done again. Doughty in *Arabia Deserta* was the last to do it effectively : but he was writing of the East as a geographer and explorer, and the style fitted well enough with the genius of the place and the man. But there are virtues here that you can cultivate : clarity, precision of outline, economy of substance, and the graces of the cadence.

We have spoken of the cadence before. Actually it is the rhythmical arrangement of the end of a sentence, and may be likened to a resolution of chords in music. It grew from Latin,

[1] Acts, xxvii, 27–29.
[2] *A Discourse of the Plantation of the Southerne Colony in Virginia by the English.* Captain John Smith's *Works*, ed. Arber.

in which language it has very definite prosodic laws. English cadences are a shadow of the Latin, less rigid and more complicated. I am not going to tell you of their structure. The early Translators, and those who wrote our liturgies, were strongly influenced by the Latin cadences that they found in the Mass and in the Vulgate. But this much is certain : that the cadence has an important effect on the *acceptability* of a statement merely by the impression of completeness and finality that its rhythm can give. Our speech still carries many of the Bible's proverbs, and perhaps something of its *tourneurs de phrase* : and yet many of us are entirely unaware either of the source or setting of the expressions that we use. Few of us could give the source of Shylock's cry " A Daniel come to judgment ! " or of " He that toucheth pitch shall be defiled " or of " Let us crown ourselves with rosebuds before they be withered : " or of " Great is truth and strong above all things." We grow impatient of the liturgical monotonies, and never reflect that these have something of the quality of the wind or the waves. We do not see that the very inaccuracies of the Bible as a narrative, the concern of the writers for their normal lessons above mere historical accuracy, give the Bible a quality of timelessness, as of a poet writing. And it is fitting to quote the tribute to it of a scientist and a sceptic : [1]

> Consider the great historical fact that, for three centuries, this book has been woven into the life of all that is best and noblest in English history ; that it has become the national epic of Britain, and is as familiar to noble and simple, from John-o'-Groat's to Land's End, as Dante and Tasso once were to Italians ; that it is written in the noblest and purest English, and abounds in exquisite beauties of pure literary form ; and finally that it forbids the veriest hind who never left his village to be ignorant of the existence of other countries and other civilizations, and of a great past stretching back to the furthest limits of the oldest civilizations of the world.

[1] Thomas Huxley : quoted by G. G. Coulton, *Medieval Panorama : The Open Bible.*

CHAPTER VIII

Satire : and the Way of a Romantic

I

I HAVE deliberately set these two, Pope and de la Mare, against each other, for the sake of contrast. The passage from Pope is satire, written in the so-called heroic couplet. It is the product of a narrow, brilliant age, compact in its social fabric, an age that dealt much in gossip, rumour, scandal ; an age when the power of a pamphleteer or satirist was to be reckoned with seriously by governments and ministers ; in which the latest witty epigram, scurrilous or complimentary, would run like a flame round the coffee-houses and clubs.

We have little satire to-day : partly because our society is too diffuse, partly because of the law of libel, partly because most of us are too busy to hate violently and long, but most of all because our hatred has so little effect. Chesterton might satirize F. E. Smith, or a lady of quality, and Belloc might attack Coulton of St. John's as the ' remote and ineffectual don ' (the last thing, of course, that Coulton ever could be) but the poetic satirist is nearly dead. Only Roy Campbell, lonely and violent, seems to have defied the custom of to-day and attacked personalities in print. Here is a sample of his writing of a more general type ; part of a character sketch of a modern poet.

> No cruel War was midwife to his state,
> No youthful accident had warped his fate,
> His feelings worked upon no Freudian plan
> In which the child is father to the " Nan ",
> Nor would he dogmatise his pet perversions
> With psycho-analytical assertions.

His sexual foundations were not laid
In the Scout Movement or the Church Brigade,
He had no high ideals or moral saws
With which to break the old Hebraic laws,
With Edward Carpenter he had no patience
Nor from the " Sonnets " would he make quotations,
No Lesbian governess had got the start of him
Or tampered early with the female part of him :
Even his misdemeanours, the most sooty,
Were more of a diversion than a duty :
He was not even member of some Church-
Society for sexual research,
Like Bertrand Russell or the wise MacCarthy—
For frowsiness his disrespect was hearty :
He read no text-books : took himself for granted
And often did precisely what he wanted :
Taking his pleasures in and out of season,
He gave for his perversity no reason,
But leaped alive (as you have seen) in rhyme
And forged ahead to have a happy time.

Now the couplet, the ten-syllable line rhymed in pairs, seems
to be a particularly suitable vehicle for this business of satire.
There appears to be a supreme finality of assertion implicit in
the structure ; the mechanism slides and clicks at the end like a
rifle-bolt going home. We say, of the statement in a good
couplet, ' This must be so and not otherwise '—however
scurrilous, lying, improbable—because of the sheer neatness of
the statement. The insect is transfixed on the pin, and twirls
helplessly round it.

There is also in the couplet at its best, as in this passage from
Pope,[1] a curious internal balance, which also contributes to this
sense of finality. Consider the first two lines :

> Peace to all such ! but were there One whose fires
> True Genius kindles, and fair Fame inspires ;

[1] Printed in full in Appendix I.

—you have a balance between *True* and *fair*,
Genius and *Fame*,
kindles and *inspires*.
A kind of impetus is given to the last four words by the alliteration, *fair Fame*—and the light ' i ' of *kindles* is picked up and clenched by the long ' i ' of *inspires*. There is a different sort of balance in the line

View him with *scornful*, yet with *jealous* eyes,

—where the first and last words balance, *scornful* and *jealous* are set against each other ; and a still more complicated kind in

Willing to wound, and yet afraid to strike,

where you have a kind of diagonal relationship, thus :

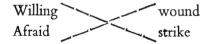

where *willing* and *wound* are linked by the *w*'s, *willing* and *afraid* are set against each other as *ideas*, and *wound* and *strike* are related in the physical intention, and yet deny each other in the line.

Now the object of Pope's attack was Addison of the *Spectator* : harmless enough, a one-time friend ; and (as with much of Pope's satire) one suspects him of being prepared to sacrifice friendship to the joy of this ' narrow and viperish utterance '. Perhaps more famous is the attack on Lord Hervey,[1] in which, it has been said, Pope ' seems to be actually screaming with malignant fury '. Listen to it :

> Let *Sporus* tremble—A. What ? that thing of silk,
> *Sporus*, that mere white curd of Ass's milk ?
> Satire or sense, alas ! can *Sporus* feel ?
> Who breaks a butterfly upon the wheel ?
> P. Yet let me flap this bug with gilded wings,
> This painted child of dirt, that stinks and stings . . .

---

[1] *Epistle to Dr. Arbuthnot.*

Watch the incredible compression. Sporus is the courtier—
gilded (remember *Lear*)—and then a bug—with gilded wings
for his wealth. He is a bed-bug, that *stinks* and *stings* ; and
the venom of the alliterative *s's* tends to mask for us the
implications of the words. He is a kind of composite insect :
the haunter of beds : *stinking* before, and after, he is crushed
by the nail : stinking as he stings, stinging as he stinks. The
images fill up the mould of the couplet like molten lead :

> . . . Whose buzz the witty and the fair annoys,
> Yet wit ne'er tastes, and beauty ne'er enjoys :
> So well-bred spaniels civilly delight
> In mumbling of the game they dare not bite.

So it goes on ; invective at white heat, under perfect control,
and with the seeming inevitability, the sense of having been
conceived and born in this identical shape. (In point of fact
it was—as nearly all poetry is—the product of incessant care
for technique, polished and re-polished, till all trace of artifice
disappears.)

There is another feature of this kind of writing that you
will meet from time to time. It is the satirist's trick of
implying judgments of value by setting two things in a particular relationship in the couplet ; we might call it the ' irony
of co-planar surfaces '. Examples are given below.

2

You will see that I have put a problem to you. If satire can
win acceptance of its most outrageous statements, by reason of
this strange sense of finality that high technique can give, may
not all poetry be open to the same indictment ? It is an old
one : the poet says *the thing that is not* ; he is the father of lies :
he misleads us by playing on our emotions.

There is some truth in all this. The poet, like any other artist,
can mislead. He can, perhaps, win acceptance for the lie. That

is why it is essential to weigh your judgments carefully : to make certain that what you are accepting *into* yourself, as it were, has stood the test of time, and that you, as an individual, are weighing what you read against your own values. Again, the test is in the wearing qualities, in the power to continue to carry significance. Pope does not, and does not intend, to deal with deeper things. But his poetry is an index to one aspect of a way of thought which is only five generations behind us. It explains much of the achievement of the eighteenth century, and of its limitations too. Its formal qualities are exquisite ; and it remains the model for all who attempt (within the limitations of our social conventions) to write satire to-day.

> The hungry judges soon the sentence sign,
> And wretches hang that jurymen may dine.

or

> And stain her honour, or her new brocade,
> Forget her prayers, or miss a masquerade.

or

> Not louder shrieks to pitying Heav'n are cast,
> When husbands, or when lap-dogs breathe their last.

For a final example, there is the notorious line that refers to Lady Mary Wortley Montagu,

> Pox'd by her love, or libell'd by her hate

which for sheer compression of vituperation, and capacity to expand in the mind, has never been equalled. But no one would dare publish such a line now.

3

I put before you this poem of de la Mare's deliberately, aware that its statement is probably against your temper, and that of your age. You may well classify it with the kind of poetry that is lightly dismissed as ' escapist ', out of touch with reality and with your experience. I am suggesting that this kind is still worth your consideration: the more so because, having been the friend of de la Mare, I am certain that he is the most genuine and least affected of all the poets I have met; and that, to him, the strange twilight world of wonder with which so much of his verse is concerned is intensely real.

Here is the poem : I give it without comment, asking you, first, to notice only the extreme delicacy of the unusual rhythm : itself an unfailing indication of the state of mind of the poet.

> What lovely things
>   Thy hand hath made :
> The smooth-plumed bird
>   In its emerald shade,
> The seed of the grass,
>   The speck of stone
> Which the wayfaring ant
>   Stirs—and hastes on !
>
> Though I should sit
>   By some tarn in thy hills,
> Using its ink
>   As the spirit wills
> To write of Earth's wonders,
>   Its live, willed things,
> Flit would the ages
>   On soundless wings
> Ere unto Z
>   My pen drew nigh ;
> Leviathan told,
>   And the honey-fly :
> And still would remain
>   My wit to try—
> My worn reeds broken,
>   The dark tarn dry,
> All words forgotten—
>   Thou, Lord, and I.

As you have gathered, I want to use this poem as a text for a discussion of the Romantic viewpoint.

There are, historically, two great roads of approach to the knowledge of the spirit of the universe.[1]

The first is the way of negation : the denial, or casting out, of all thoughts except those of the numinous or divine. This is the way of the ascetic, as St. Thomas à Kempis knew : ' In solitude and in silence the devout soul advances with speedy steps, and learns the hidden truths of God. There, she finds the fountain of tears, in which she bathes and purifies herself every night : there, she riseth to a more intimate union with her Creator, in proportion as she leaves the darkness, impurity and tumult of the world.'[2] In the light of the great Eastern religions such a statement is not to be dismissed hurriedly ; all that we can say is that it presents intense difficulty for those who attempt to practise it to-day.

The second is the way of affirmation ; the acceptance of the creative universe and the approach to divinity through the cultivation, first of a sense of awe at the universe, and then through that awe of a sense of unity with the world. Now I do not suggest that you must postulate in your consideration of this the acceptance of a traditional God, or of Paley's Watch-maker, or of the Great Mathematician. What I am suggesting is that the sense of awe experienced by the astronomer, or of the atomic physicist, is no different in its ultimate quality from that of the saint or mystic. The emotions of Sir Thomas Browne are not, in *essence*, different from those of the observer at Mt. Palomar confronting the first photograph of the nebulae on the scale that the new mirror has made possible. There is still the struggle of the human mind to begin to realize this immensity, and we can recall Sir Thomas Browne's advice : ' Acquaint thyself with the choragium of the stars. . . . Have a glimpse of incomprehensibles, and Thoughts of things, which Thoughts but tenderly touch.'

Now the prelude to the coming of this sense of wonder is a

[1] I am indebted for the formulation which follows to Charles Williams, *The Figure of Beatrice.*   [2] *Imitation of Christ*, xx.

93

physical awareness of the *detail* of life about one : not merely of natural objects but of buildings, of people, of pictures. The cultivation of this awareness *for its own sake* is the way of the aesthete, and leads ultimately to sterility. If it is used rightly, it results in a curious and often sudden perception of scale in the world. I have known men emerging from a long psychological illness suddenly become aware of the beauty of trivial things— of hedge grasses, wild flowers, thistles ; it was as if some kind of film had been removed from their eyes. (Incidentally, have you ever lain down in a hayfield, your face among the roots of the grass, and seen that incredible microcosmic life that goes on in the jungle there ?)

There is a famous picture by Crome, of the East Anglian school, called *Thistle and Water Vole*. It is no more than the grasses and a thistle, beside a Fen river, a tiny fragment of the bank with its water and rotten camp-sheathing (such as Constable loved to paint) with a vole beside ; and yet the whole is full of a miraculous insight into this life of the microcosm, vivid, exciting, and in some way, full of healing.

So it was that at the end of *The Ancient Mariner* spiritual relief came when the Mariner blessed the water-snakes. Notice how their detail was suddenly perceived *inwardly*, as it were :

> Within the shadow of the ship
> I watch'd their rich attire :
> Blue, glossy green, and velvet black,
> They coil'd and swam ; and every track
> Was a flash of golden fire.
>
> O happy living things ! no tongue
> Their beauty might declare :
> A spring of love gush'd from my heart,
> And I bless'd them unaware :
> Sure my kind saint took pity on me,
> And I bless'd them unaware.

He blesses them *unaware* : for now there has been achieved an

CROME: *Thistle and Water Vole*

unconscious liberation of his own personality, the resolution of his sense of guilt. So Wordsworth, remembering the daffodils seen by the lake :

> For oft, when on my couch I lie
>   In vacant or in pensive mood,
> They flash upon that inward eye
>   Which is the bliss of solitude ;
> And then my heart with pleasure fills,
> And dances· with the daffodils.

So Yeats (though the poem is more complex ; for the image in the last verse is the Annunciation-image, of a ray of light coming down from heaven and entering the *ear* of the Virgin : the Light and the Word)

> Through intricate motions ran
> Stream and gliding sun
> And all my heart seemed gay :
> Some stupid thing that I had done
> Made my attention stray.
>
> Repentance keeps my heart impure ;
> But what am I that dare
> Fancy that I can
> Better conduct myself or have more
> Sense than a common man ?
>
> What motion of the sun or stream
> Or eyelid shot the gleam
> That pierced my body through ?
> What made me live like these that seem
> Self-born, born anew ? [1]

The process is, I repeat, one of the perception of scale ; and, as a logical step beyond that, the perception of one's relationship to the universe in a positive sense : the acceptance of the currents of life. Blake put it in his own crude and violent fashion :

> Great things are done when men and mountains meet :
> This is not done by jostling in the street.

---

[1] *Stream and Sun at Glendalough.*

and in a more difficult form, not easily to be grasped at first hearing :

> Mock on, mock on, Voltaire, Rousseau
> Mock on, mock on ; 'tis all in vain !
> You throw the sand against the wind,
> And the wind throws it back again.
>
> And every sand becomes a gem
> Reflected in the beams divine ;
> Blown back they blind the mocking eye,
> But still in Israel's paths they shine.
>
> The Atoms of Democritus
> And Newton's Particles of Light
> Are sands upon the Red Sea shore,
> Where Israel's tents do shine so bright.

Now turn again to the de la Mare poem. It is very simple : little more than a statement of wonder at the infiniteness of the created world. There are some details worth your notice ; the contrast between the soft vowels of *smooth-plumed* and the hardness of *emerald shade* ; the way in which *tarn*, the black water in the small deep mountain lake is carried forward to *ink* ; the inversion and hover [1] of

> flit woùld the àges

to give the suggestion of wing-beats. The line *ere unto Z* is the Biblical reference, Alpha and Omega ; as is Leviathan and the honey-fly, from Proverbs or Job. The poem is on a note of humility and piety. It has something in it of the quiet peace of some of the seventeenth-century religious poets : the peace that comes from a certainty of their relationship to the Creator and his creatures. Read the Introduction to Blake's *Songs of Innocence*.

One dare not dogmatize. It is proper, however, to ask ourselves whether it may not be that the emotion of awe is a necessary condition of spiritual growth ? Thinking, as we

[1] Hover : a missed beat : Flìt . . . would the ages.

question, of the effects upon humanity of the attitude opposed to awe ; and, furthermore, whether a secondary stage following on such awe is not (as Wordsworth found it to be) an insight into the heart of things. It is, I think, a pity if, by reason of cynicism, or materialism, or certainty as to our own self-sufficiency, we turn our backs on the way of the Romantic, which leads us through humility to wonder and then to ecstasy. All these abstractions (and particularly that last word *ecstasy*) are of course no more than approximations to what we are trying to convey. The experience is incommunicable, save through the artist's creation itself.

Notes for
A Background to English Literary History
I
(c. 1300–1660)

I

IN the preceding lectures I have tried to suggest some methods
of approaching isolated pieces of prose and verse. In these last
two lectures I am going to try to give you a picture (in the
broadest outline) of English literary history. All that I can do is
to suggest some impressions of what seem to me the larger
rhythms and movements in time. I want you to see these in
terms of the facts—dates and so on—in the pamphlet [1] which
you have before you. You will see that the left-hand column
contains the names of the more important authors, and their
dates. In the next are the titles of works—one or two, but
usually not more—which will serve, if you like, as starting-
points for going more deeply into each particular author. Or,
from another point of view, you would, if you read all these
works, have a background of knowledge that many professional
students of literature would be glad to possess.

You will notice that I have left out Shakespeare, for whom
there is ample guidance available elsewhere.

In the right-hand column I have set out a number of events,
chosen from as wide a range as possible, which are roughly
contemporaneous with the writings. Some of these are political
or constitutional, some social or architectural, or scientific ; but
I have selected each one as illuminating, in some sense, the writer
and his period, or symbolizing, in a direct or oblique manner,
the great movements in the thought of his time. For it is

[1] Reproduced as Appendix II, p. 157.

essential that you should see literature as reflecting, affirming, or (on occasion) denying the spirit of its age.

I have also given an arbitrary list of some twenty books [1] which I would like each one of you to have at your bedside : together with a few anthologies which seem to me satisfying. The choice is, of course, both arbitrary and personal ; but the page has been left with wide margins so that you can jot down your own additions. The one thing you must *not* say is, " Oh, I won't have time to read any of this." Most careers have in them, at some stage or other, long periods of waiting on events. You can read all you want to in those times, provided only that you are ready. In this sense, you have all time before you, though you will (if you are wise) never be satisfied or know finality. All that you and I are doing now is to examine the charts and maps for the future ; but those charts and maps are part of the essential equipment. Your plan, as I see it, is to ' mark down ' in this first survey anything that attracts you in any period ; to acquire a sense of perspective over the periods as a whole ; to learn to browse till you have decided where your tastes are likely to lie ; and finally to reach that most exciting stage when things ' begin to fit '. By that I mean that you will begin to discover a sense of continuity in literature, to find events of history, sociology, art, music, architecture ; all supporting, clarifying, enriching, what you read. And when you reach that stage the excitement and its illumination increases with a strange and almost terrifying momentum.

2

I spoke just now of maps and charts ; and I want to return for a moment to that image. If you look at the map of Europe that is before you, you can see the great travel routes of thought and literature swinging northwards from the Mediterranean— Egypt to Greece ; Palestine to Greece ; Greece to Sicily ;

[1] Appendix III, p. 161.

Sicily northwards to Rome. In Rome the eddy circles for a while, and then, by some queer trick, goes underground to rise again in Constantinople, which preserves, miraculously, what is left of both Roman and Hellenic civilization. Constantinople in its turn falls to the Turkish invaders, and the current follows the trade route up the Adriatic to North Italy, to found there the classical humanism which is to determine, by and large, the thought of Europe for the next four hundred years. From North Italy it goes up the Rhone Valley, the traditional highway for culture, or trade, or war, to Paris : spreading as it goes, both east and west. And here it is joined by a wide circling current, which has flowed from Arabia and Egypt, through Morocco, across the straits to Spain, and thus across into France, into North Italy. It is that of the Arabic Commentators on Aristotle, and the mathematical and physical studies preserved and developed by the Moorish civilization. It crosses to England : moving, as it were, in rhythmic impulses of its current, impulses which are given by political events, or the breaching of dams by the efforts of single men : scholars, reformers, princes.

For a time the tide flows strongly in the one direction, bringing to us nearly everything on which our traditions, and even our civilization, are based. We may remind ourselves of some of them : the Christian tradition, itself absorbing and consolidating what was most stable in Hebraic and Hellenic thought ; science, mathematics, and astronomy from Egypt, Arabia, Greece ; law and the science of government from Rome ; painting from Italy ; architecture from that curious eddy in Northern France which we call the Gothic. In three successive centuries these waves of thought reach England, all, or nearly all, from the south : following, as always, the routes of trade.[1] And when they have reached it, the waters grow calmer, and blend with other

[1] I am well aware that this is an unjust simplification ; the Anglo-Saxon tradition is a great and important one. Consider, for example, R. W. Chambers' *On the Continuity of English Prose*. But for the perception of a pattern at this stage, the scaffolding must be arbitrary and even crude ; to be replaced by more elaborate structures at a later stage of knowledge.

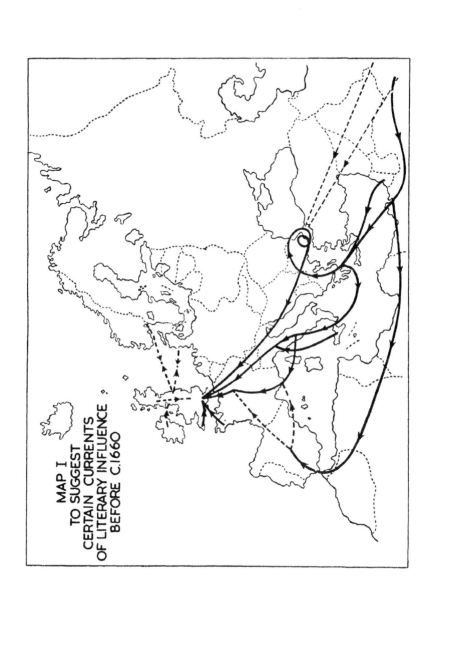

MAP I
TO SUGGEST
CERTAIN CURRENTS
OF LITERARY INFLUENCE
BEFORE C.1660

waters in our strange and complicated racial heritage. Not until the eighteenth century are we aware of a counter-current setting from the north ; bringing with it the Celtic and Gaelic influences which combine (with other things) to produce what we term Romanticism.

This, perhaps, for the broadest picture ; remembering that every generalization is valid only for so long as it takes us to examine the parts more closely and to perceive, as we must do, the imprecision of the first outline. That, in literary history, is an inevitable process ; our apprehension of it is a growth, with all the changes that growth implies ; and for a time, as we read, the picture will grow confused with so many exceptions, so much complexity at different levels beneath the surface. We must think, continually, of the economic and political factors behind events, and how they affect men's writing ; and, as always in literature, we must remember that the roots of any so-called ' movement ' always go deeper, behind and beyond the dates at which text-books would have us believe they start. ' Schools ' and ' movements ' are convenient concepts for the initial framework ; but the further they are analysed the more unsatisfactory they appear to be.

That is one thought, the conception of these currents of ideas running through Europe. There is a second thought which you may find helpful. If we continue our wave-simile, it looks as if each ' age ' may be thought of as a wave that gathers height and momentum, and poises for a moment, in the shallower water, before it breaks. A tradition in art or government, a form in architecture or in verse, reaches its moment of perfection. Then, for many reasons—perhaps because the tension is too acute, or because the drive of the groundswell behind it is fading, and the water has grown shallow, or because men are mistaking the means for the end, or the letter for the law—the wave breaks, and we hear

> The rattle of pebbles on the shore
> Under the receding wave.

From another point of view, each age seems to become increasingly complex, over-organized, tense with the insolubility of its own problems. When it reaches this point, there is often an overwhelming impulse to simplify—'Back to Nature', 'Back to the Middle Ages'—or to take refuge in some religious or political formula or catchword that appears to remove the burden of responsibility from the individual, and transfers it to society as a whole. And at times it may seem as if such simplification has opened new doors upon the world : as the French Revolution seemed to have opened them to the young poets of the Romantic Revival, or as Fascism or Marxism seemed once, to some individuals, to hold the solutions of all problems. "Bliss was it in that dawn to be alive . . ."

But within this complexity of actions and reactions, of social, economic and political trends, there is, as in history, the unexplained phenomenon of the individual ; and we must remember always that literary history is, in a large measure, the lives of its writers. Good biographies are available to you on every hand ; with exceptions, notably that of Shakespeare. Of him we know little, and tend, therefore, to make a composite picture from among the images of his characters. As you read the biographies, you will, I think, be faced with certain paradoxes. First, the discrepancy, which is often considerable, between the life and the work, between the ideals put forward in the writing, and the record of the life lived. Very few writers have lived up to Milton's precept :

> And long it was not after, when I was confirmed in this opinion, that he who would not be frustrate of his hope to write well hereafter in laudable things, ought himself to be a true poem ; that is, a composition and pattern of the best and honourablest things ; not presuming to sing high praises of heroic men, or famous cities, unless he have in himself the experience and practice of all that which is praiseworthy.

Let us be frank : few writers stand the test. Chaucer was an efficient civil servant ; Milton a great First Secretary of the Commonwealth ; Donne, in his later years, perhaps the greatest preacher in the language ; Swift " served "—though in his own tortuous fashion—" human liberty ". Against these we must set a long record of the artist or poet or writer as the irritable, capricious figure, finding difficulty in adjusting himself to his age or to the codes of society; the victim of sudden enthusiasms, of melancholia, of instability of mood, at times of a deep and level pessimism. Sir Philip Sidney, ' that white-flamed soul ', might die at Zutphen, and Byron (who would merit that description less) at Missolonghi : but the deaths of the poets, as their lives, make curious reading.

There is no answer : and the Philistine or the logician can always ask the poet, as Plato does, " What cities have *you* founded ? " But in this discrepancy, the lack of correspondence between the life and the work, the case of the artist is, I believe, no different from that which we are apt to find in the biographies of the soldier, the politician, the leaders or rulers of the people. It is only that his inmost life is more available to us, and we dissect it with greater zeal. By his function the artist will be intensely sensitive, and therefore is apt to be vain and irritable. He will be in advance of his time, aware of its shortcomings, and therefore in rebellion against it and the conditions which it imposes upon him. His energies will be narrowed into a single channel, and for this reason, he will probably fail to make many of the normal adjustments to daily life. And finally his whole life will be a ceaseless conflict to express, through endless shaping of intractable material, his own special vision. He knows that, however well he shapes it, it will never be more than an approximation to what he sees.

Remember these things when you read literary biographies ; and remember Shakespeare :

> Use every man after his desert, and who should 'scape whipping ?

The first section on your pamphlet at which I want to glance for a moment extends to the Restoration, 1660. You will see that I have started, paradoxically enough, with three Italians, Dante, Boccaccio, and Petrarch. They come first because we must, I think, consider them as the beginning of European literature, and because English is perpetually and extensively in debt to all three and to their forerunners. Dante is available to us in many excellent translations. It is arguable that *The Divine Comedy* is, with the *Iliad* and *Paradise Lost*, among the greatest works of the human imagination.

Against the early history of the period the great tradition of English drama develops ; starting with religious ritual, those imitating the events of the Birth : passing from church to churchyard, and those beyond the control of the Church, to ' ways and greens ', till by the middle of the fourteenth century the guilds stage their plays or crude pageants in the great market towns. There is the impact upon the country of the Black Death, with its enormous mortality, and a break-up of the whole social fabric in consequence ; and the unrest which follows culminates in the Peasants' Revolt. In this century you will find a mirror of life, and of social history, in Chaucer and Langland. Both have been popularized by broadcasting, and both are available in modernized versions, so that the language need be no deterrent. Of the ' God's plenty ' that is in Chaucer, the brilliance and subtlety of his colour portraits, his humour, and his wisdom, many have written. It is enough to remind you that the debt of English poets to him is great and constant. And at some time or other you should look into Malory, for many writers after are deeply in his debt also. You will find him in this simple, incisive prose, strung upon conjunctions, admirably fitted to the magical, erratic characters of the narrative. And if you want to understand it further, there are two books—poles apart—that you may one day read: C. S. Lewis' *The Allegory of Love*, and T. H. White's *The Sword in the Stone*;[1] the latter a vivid and delightful account of the boyhood of King Arthur.

Of the group known as the Scottish Chaucerians, I have suggested only Henryson, for his version of the Cressida story, and for the Fables in the manner of La Fontaine ; and Dunbar for a single poem, *Lament for the Makaris*, for the dead poets of the past. I have suggested this because it seems to me to contain in essence one great characteristic of medieval poetry, the fear and sorrow before death :

> I that in heill was and gladnèss
> Am trublit now with great sicknesse
> And feblit with infirmitie :—
> > *Timor Mortis conturbat me.*

For with all their gaiety, all their conventions of May mornings and the Coming of Spring, a great shadow hung over the mind of man. Perhaps it can be expressed most simply in two texts :

> The wages of sin is death.
> If we say that we have no sin we deceive ourselves,
> and the truth is not in us.

Therefore the sense of life and death are each sharpened by that dichotomy : bawdry, drunkenness, piety, the threat of hell-fire made vivid in a dozen different ways, are intensified by the shadow of the skeleton, the Dance of Death (consider Holbein's version) that was spread throughout Europe.

4

Meanwhile, Constantinople has fallen, and the scholars with their classical manuscripts, the artists with the traditions of their craft, are dispersed to North Italy, where a new civilization is rising to civilize in its turn the whole of Europe. (You need not, I think, pay much attention to those who deny that there is any valid use or meaning for the term Renaissance : and sooner or later you should read Walter Pater's book of that name.)

[1] Now part of *The Once and Future King*

The results of this humanism are infinitely complicated. All I want to suggest now is two main effects. Firstly, classical humanism, imported into England in the mid-sixteenth century, is to determine the whole course of English education for three hundred years and more. It becomes a kind of reference-point, a norm, and a source for almost anything that is good, and for not a little that is bad, in our cultural tradition. Only in the last half-century, perhaps in the last thirty years, have we thrown that tradition aside. So tremendous was the power of the classical tradition that much of the critical writing of the later sixteenth century is occupied with the problem of how far, and in what manner, English can be adapted to classical structures and metres. Those questions (which were, as always, solved in practice by the good sense of the writers themselves, and by the native traditions which they inherited) were most bitter over the matter of language. The rate of change in vocabulary, structure, pronunciation of English, had been extremely rapid ; if it was to continue (so men argued) serious philosophical or scientific writing might become obsolete a hundred years after it was written. Remember that Latin was the international language of Europe ; as it still is of the Roman Church. The medieval student was free of every university in Europe because the lectures were in Latin. It was the language of theology, law, science, biology, ethics, astronomy, mathematics. Until after Milton's time it was the language of diplomacy. Between 1540 and 1660 English is, as it were, on trial. Could it absorb from Greek and Latin the complex and abstract vocabulary which the growth of science demanded; draw from classical sources the overtones that it required to express itself ; and, lacking case-endings and inflections, develop a sentence of sufficient weight and complexity to meet the new demands ? (As a measure of how deeply the Latin tradition was embedded in this country, we can think of the Elizabethan schoolboy, committed to a long and rigorous discipline of reading, writing letters to his parents, in very tolerable Latin, at the age of nine or ten.)

English proved itself capable of meeting these new demands : but from, say, 1540 to 1660 the issue must have seemed in doubt.

This process of absorption, of nationalization, of adaptation, is common to many forms. During the sixteenth century the sonnet and the lyric emerge ; you can still read Wyatt's and Surrey's lyrics with pleasure, though many of them are taken from the French or Italian. (Remember, in passing, that very little literature, or painting, or architecture, or music, is *original* in any absolute sense. Every age borrows and adapts.) You can see Surrey forging the first English blank verse. People are translating, with a growing sense of excitement, from French and Italian, and above all from the Latin authors. There are the great treatises by Ascham on two central subjects of the age, archery and education, and the last is important if you wish to understand how Elizabethan education grew : for in this century most of the English Grammar Schools are founded, and the school system starts to take its characteristic shape, which is not to be destroyed, finally, till 1945. Something like a philosophy of government is evolving, and the process of evolution is accelerated through a troubled century of many reigns, to take a fairly modern form—even from our view-point to-day—in the thought of the later seventeenth century. The Elizabethan Voyagers (and there is a vast and exciting literature here—Hakluyt, Frobisher, Captain John Smith, accounts of the economics of colonization and the traffics and discoveries of the New World) show that the life of action could produce a strong and efficient prose, well suited to narrative. You can see it at its best in the accounts of the sea-voyages in the Acts of the Apostles. Then you have the story of the Armada ; the glory of the Elizabethan Court ; an England at last united, and vigorous and free : an England in which everyone burst out singing ; an age that achieved the humanist ideal, where every man might be courtier, soldier, scholar, and write and die as Sidney died. Don't believe it—altogether : rather learn to look, in this as in every age, for the other side of the medal. Think sometimes that the age of Shakespeare saw the first highly organized and efficient secret service : think of a Court riddled with corruption, thronged with suitors whose way to the throne was only cleared by lavish bribery (if you want evidence of what the Court, or the law-courts were like, go to Shakespeare) ; think of a populace that (for all the exquisite Elizabethan songs) tolerated and enjoyed the utmost brutality in their sports, their asylums, their executions; think of a London that was never (as Morris thought it was in the Middle Ages) 'small and white and clean', but a city in which the Puritan believed (with some reason) that the periodical visitations of the plague were the judgment of God upon its wickedness.

And yet massive work is being done everywhere. Spenser's *Faerie Queene* is at once the last spark from the fading Arthurian legend, and the great pseudo-epic that brought English into competition—by its sheer vastness of scale—with Tasso and Ariosto ; that showed triumphantly how a single mind could blend allegory, and politics, and romance, and moralizing, and a frank pleasure in the delighted senses. It was a fairy-tale : yet Spenser, exiled in Ireland, is conscious of the growing excitement as the ships come into London River with stories of countries as strange as fairyland, new-discovered :

> Who ever heard of th' Indian Peru ?
> Or who in venturous vessel measurèd
> The Amazon huge river, now found true ?
> Or fruitfullest Virginia who did ever view ? [1]

So Othello might ensnare Desdemona with his stories of

> the Anthropophagi, and men whose heads
> Do grow beneath their shoulders. [2]

and the news of shipping was urgent to the London citizen as it was to Antonio and Shylock on the Rialto.

[1] *Faerie Queene*, ii, Induction.   [2] *Othello*, i, 3.

Shakespeare bridges the gap between the two ages. Most of his best work is Jacobean. And now the theatre grows more complex, more elaborate in its stage devices, and technique of the Masque, more intricate in the analysis of its characters, more horrific in the plots of its tragedies. At the same time, but slowly, the fashion of lyric poetry changes : from the conventional love poetry which we call Petrarchan, with its stereotyped adornment of the beloved, and its melancholy lovers (watch them being parodied in *As You Like It*, in *Much Ado*, and above all in the highly topical *Love's Labour's Lost*) and we see the development of the style called 'Metaphysical'. The temper of the age is changing, and though we can give many reasons for this change, we do not understand them all.

In the broadest outline it seems as if men were sorting out, and reconsidering the values of, the treasures which the Renaissance had showered upon them. All knowledge was man's province : and a restless, excited, curious age, that seemed to set no limits to man's conquests, is perhaps best symbolized by Holbein's *The Ambassadors*. In that picture, which you can see in the National Gallery, you have an emblem of the time : the two men with their poise and arrogance, in their richly decorated clothes ; the table covered with every variety of scientific and astronomical instrument ; the musical instruments below ; the globes that symbolize the known world that they had conquered. And below it, as a grim jest by Holbein, the hollow bone that, seen from the side, shows a skull. We are aware of a series of challenges to the systems of thought and learning that had governed Europe for centuries. Men are beginning to distrust the authority of books ; for an instance we can take that vast snowball of unnatural Natural History, rolling down from the classical authors, and gathering its accretions of inaccuracies which acquire the force of authority *merely because they are written*. And you can watch that snowball being melted—a little cautiously—for he has allegiance both to the Old Learning and to the New Science—in the *Vulgar Errors* of Sir Thomas

HOLBEIN: *The Ambassadors*

Browne. You will find, I think, that Browne is for your purposes an unusually fascinating and illuminating writer ; and you will mistrust all those who tell you that he is no more than a superb but eccentric artist in high-sounding Latinized words. *Religio Medici* will give you a great deal of insight into the religious problems of the time ; and it will force you, very often, to ask yourselves the question : " Is this *true* ? " (Not, as so many professional students of literature ask : " Who influenced him, or whom did he influence ? ") His ' Science' in the *Vulgar Errors* is a strange and entertaining blend of knowledge, observation, and an emotional excitement at finding resemblance in disparates, as metaphysical poetry is concerned to do. His facts appear to be inseparable from his values ; both are discussed with a common emotional excitement. And in the *Garden of Cyrus* you will find a strange attempt to discover, in an enormous range of examples, the five-pointed figure which he called the *Quincunx* ; in which he ranges from botany to battle-formations, and from the geometry of the times to the symbolism of the Five Foolish Virgins. It is almost as if the science of the crystallographer had become inextricably confused with the British Israelites.

All sorts of things are being challenged as the New Learning develops. Mathematics, magnetism, optics, chemistry, are gathering way like ships coming out of harbour, and start to feel the sea wind at the time of the Restoration. Anatomy, physiology, and physics are developing at the hands of Harvey and Boyle. And for religion, the moderate Churchman looking back from 1620 over the previous eighty years might well be perplexed before an expanding universe, and a dogma that had changed its shape at the bidding of the King. What *is* Freedom ? (Hobbes in the *Leviathan* will try to answer that question). What was to be the relationship between Church and State ? The humanism of the Renaissance had set a warmer current flowing ; and it did not mix too well with orthodoxy. The delighted senses of Renaissance man, his moods of exaltation and depression, were meeting the cold rising tide of Puritanism. For the thought of the Renaissance is more than half-pagan ; and the bitter meeting of the tides might be thought of as Swinburne sung it, almost in our time :

Thou hast conquered, O pale Galilean ; the world has grown
    grey from thy breath ;
We have drunken of things Lethean, and fed on the fullness of
    death.
Laurel is green for a season, and love grows sweet for a day ;
But love grows bitter with treason, and laurel outlives not May.

There are questionings everywhere. What is the nature of love—of body, or of soul, or of both ? What is the significance of the divided soul of which men are becoming so terribly aware ? What are the ways of God, and how is the theologian to justify them to men ? What lies beyond the grave ? This generation is much possessed by death ; and I sometimes think that John Donne, of St. Paul's, one of the greatest preachers in our language, is forcing his vast congregation to look into the grave and its corruption so that they may be quite certain there is no salvation there and so must look upwards instead. It is an age curiously like our own : an age that is being forced to reconsider fundamental values, but lacking the coherence to do it. For whatever solidity Elizabeth gave to the period that bears her name is tending to break apart. The glory and vitality of the Court seems to have departed, and the writers are developing their genius in isolated pockets throughout England : Browne at Norwich, Burton at Oxford, Herrick in a Devonshire parsonage, with that naive mixture of devotion and sensuousness that helps us to understand the age.

The grey Puritan tides continue to rise through the first half of the century, pushing higher up the shore the little group of High Churchmen and mystics, the cavalier poets with their delicacy and grace and music, learnt from the Elizabethan yet with a poise and sense of breeding that is all their own. The king dies, and the new philosophy of government has its first exposition in practice. In the mind of Milton, half humanist and half Puritan, the greatest poem in English is developing. But in the meantime there are more urgent things for the First Secretary of the Commonwealth to do. He must defend the liberty of the Press, and the execution of his King, and undertake learned and bitter controversy in the politics of Europe. By 1652 he is blind. *Paradise Lost* is not published till 1667.

CHAPTER X

Notes for
A Background to English Literary History
II
(c. 1660–1900)

I

IN the last lecture we spoke of the great tides of thought flowing through Europe, and of the rising and breaking of individual waves. I warned you that all arbitrary dates were, in the last analysis, misleading ; since all events have long fibrous roots reaching back into the past. But if we are to select any one determining date, the Restoration of 1660 shows as clear a break as any. Within a decade, the foundation of the Royal Society, with its demands for clarity and precision in common speech, sets a new standard of English prose. The discoveries in science are bearing fruit ; the circulation of the blood, Cartesian mathematics, physics, electricity, and magnetism. Medical knowledge is developing rapidly, though man is as helpless before the Plague as he was three hundred years before. (Read, as an example of brilliant journalism of the time, Defoe's *Journal of the Plague Year* : and for a sketch of the low life of London, his *Moll Flanders*.) There is wealth, and leisure for good talk and unlimited gossip ; look at Aubrey's *Lives* as well as Pepys' *Diary*. The last of the metaphysical tradition, in poetry and the sermon, is ebbing away. The Court has brought back with it much of France, and continental travel becomes possible again on a large scale. Architects and painters turn largely to Italy, and acclimatize what they have learnt there to produce the great

114

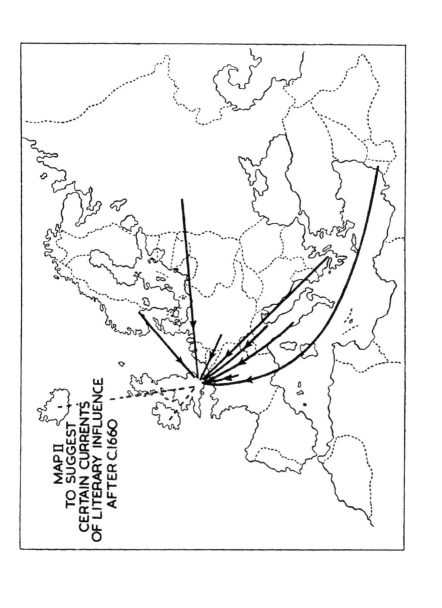

MAP II
TO SUGGEST
CERTAIN CURRENTS
OF LITERARY INFLUENCE
AFTER C.1660

age of English building. In morals there is a reaction against Puritanism ; so much so that a certain clergyman of the time, Jeremy Collier, published in 1698 *A Short View of the Profaneness and Immorality of the English Stage*, a work containing a collection of immoral passages from the plays of the previous years. What Restoration Comedy could be at its best—brilliant, witty, quick-moving, yet with considerable insight into character— you can see from the frequent revivals now. In general these plays owe a good deal to Ben Jonson's Comedy of Humours, itself a descendant of the Roman Comedy. Its characters present psychological abnormalities, which are to be shocked back into normality in the course of the play ; and their idiosyncrasies are often apparent from their names. The tragedy of the period is narrower, concerned more with the almost geometrical balancing of claims that (in themselves just) prove in certain defined circumstances to be incompatible— Love versus Honour, Love versus Patriotism, and so forth. The system of rewards and punishments seems to be in part a relic of the Puritan tradition, in part the outcome of the hard logical thought of France.

From the Restoration to the turn of the century the writers have produced some of your very best bedside reading : the Diaries of Pepys and Evelyn, Aubrey's *Brief Lives*, Walton's *Compleat Angler*. And you may watch the novel taking shape in Bunyan and Defoe, the interest in character and feeling growing from the Character Writers of the seventeenth century : those strange little thumbnail sketches of contemporary characters that are fascinating to read : *A She-Precise Hypocrite, An Unworthy Lawyer, A Fair and Happy Milkmaid*—the very titles are amusing.

The new dynasty is founded, and again the Vicar of Bray changes his form of religion. And, confronting these rapid and violent modulations of belief, men begin to look for the rational element in religion, something which the man of sense and breeding can accept, even if it be a kind of greatest common measure of the rapidly multiplying sects. Throughout the course of the eighteenth century you can see two main threads in religious thought : the urbane, well-bred, moderate, inclining to scepticism ; and the enthusiasm of nonconformity which saw the need of the people for a religion which should appeal to the heart rather than the head. But England is still intolerant, and religious disabilities are apparent everywhere.

It is an age of great architecture, based on a vivid sense of the classical tradition, and on the intelligence to modify it to northern needs. Proportion, dignity, restraint, symmetry, are ideals of the age that are best seen in the architecture of Wren, of Vanbrugh, in the city churches, in collegiate buildings of all kinds. The great political parties take shape, and with their rise literature acquires a new importance, for persuasion, propaganda, and vituperation. The Copyright Act of 1709 makes it possible for an author to live ; and London becomes thronged with writers. Pamphlets, lampoons, satires, have a market value, in cash or in preferment : and perhaps the greatest single writer in this kind is Swift. The new middle class, with increasing wealth and leisure demands news, entertainment, novelty to stir its sensibilities, moral essays to instruct it—and in particular its women : who, as always, are felt by male superiority to be in need of improving literature to correct their essential levity of mind, as well as to occupy their genteel and leisured lives. (There were arch-models in Latin literature for satirical attacks upon them.) And because, in the highly concentrated literary circles of London, gossip, scandal and good talk can circulate rapidly, satire becomes an important and highly developed art ; and one which has the double function of ministering to the writer's personal sense of superiority, and of allowing him to believe that he is effectively supporting the morality of society by attacking all departures from the well-bred rational norm that it has set up. The art of satire, following Dryden's model, achieves an exactness and compression of phrase never equalled before or since : and we may wonder (until we realize the amorphous state of the Law of Libel) how these writers got away with it. Look at the footnotes to *The Dunciad*, and see the names of Pope's contemporaries, impaled like insects there.

An urbane, narrow, Roman age : brilliant, witty, leisured : achieving (as some have held) the nearest to a completely civilized state that this country has seen. You will often meet the phrase " Our Excellent and Indispensable Eighteenth Century ", and among the Queen Anne houses, the exquisite formal gardens, the dignified monuments with their Latin epitaphs and their Roman Urns, you will see what the phrase means. But there is another side to it, as always ; and that side you may see most easily in the drawings of Hogarth (the nearest approach to certain of the strip-cartoons of our day) that show us the life of London in the first half of the century. Like the Elizabethan, it is a coarse, violent world of rakes and harlots in their moral progress from prosperity to destruction : of Gin Lane and Beer Street, and the appalling mortality from drink, overcrowding, quack doctors ; of prisons where rogues and debtors, guilty and innocent, died together of gaol fever. It is an age of sycophants, of political jobbery, of vast retinues in the great houses, of profligates like Colonel Chartres whose epitaph is at once an indication of his reputation and a magnificent example of the incisiveness and weight of eighteeenth-century prose style :

Here continueth to rot,
the body of FRANCIS CHARTRES ;
who, with an INFLEXIBLE CONSTANCY, and
INIMITABLE UNIFORMITY of life,
PERSISTED,
in spite of AGE and INFIRMITIES
in the practice of EVERY HUMAN VICE
excepting PRODIGALITY and HYPOCRISY.
His insatiable AVARICE exempted him from the first ;
his matchless IMPUDENCE from the second.

But the century moves on ; as always, against a background of wars and political events, the rise and fall of ministries ; two rebellions and three great campaigns, but none close enough to England to affect the whole life of a people. And because there is wealth and leisure, and no great pressure from without until the Napoleonic wars, literature spreads out into broad lakes, with backwaters leading from them, where the " dilettanti " can amuse themselves to their hearts' content. The poets turn to landscape and nature in verse that can be related to the great landscape painters of the period : Dyer to Wilson, Cowper to Girtin, Crabbe to Morland. It is the age of the landscape gardener, of ' classical ' effects in little Greek temples in the grounds of the great houses, of Chinese pagodas, of mock ' Gothick ' buildings, of the connoisseur and the scholar. There is leisure for the great novels with their slow deliberate development of plot and character, which recently caused several of the greatest writers to head the list of works voted (in the United States) to be the ' dullest ' in literature. Literature is still centred in London, where there are coffee houses, and good talk, and a great and eccentric personality like Johnson's can make itself felt throughout the country.

Johnson's exploration of Scotland (and remember that his *Journey to the Western Islands of Scotland* is an excellent bedside book) can be taken as in some sense a symbol of the changing interest in the world. For at the turn of the century the tide (to keep our first image) seems to turn, or at least one tidal current starts to set from the North. It is difficult to define it exactly, but we can attempt to consider it in terms of what the French critic, Taine, saw as the basic determining factors of literature—race, environment, time. For in general that literature which comes from the North has the qualities of vagueness (as in a land of mist and rain), a certain melancholy (for the life is hard and the soil unfruitful) and a fear of the unknown and of nature that is often terrible and menacing. It brought into English the Gaelic and the Celtic moods : both subject to alternating depression and exaltation, aware of the supernatural in a land where ' gliding ghosts ' might be discerned through the rain that swept across the moors, and where the kings might rise from their burial mounds at night in the ancient churchyard of Iona. The Scottish Ballad is rediscovered through Percy's *Reliques*, and brings with it the strange wild elegiac note that we heard in *The Twa Corbies*, or in that tiny fragment of a love-poem :

> O Western Wind when wilt thou blow
>   That the small rain down can rain ?
> Christ, that my love were in my arms
>   And I in my bed again ! [1]

At first the supernatural is perceived, as it were, only from the outside : men are titillating themselves with the thought of the romantic ruin by moonlight, or the ' wild and heathy scene ', but they are not living it. Later, the sense of wonder, uncertainty, awe, will become a part of life ; for the moment the poets are content to write of the Popular Superstitions of the Scottish Highlands, as Collins did, or to think of their past in the history of the Druids. And for a brief moment it seemed as if they might turn their faces northward, away from Greece, to a kind of Scottish Homer, Ossian, whose poems were allegedly translated by a Scottish schoolmaster, James Macpherson. But that story is one of the fairy-tales of English literary history.

2

It is a mistake to suggest that the eighteenth century is wholly an age of prose or of satire, or even of ' Reason '. Much nature poetry is being written, and the antithesis between town and country, which appears at the Restoration in the verse of Otway,

---

[1] This is Gummere's version. Consider that given by Chambers and Sidgwick for the changed rhythm—and meaning :

> Western wind, when will thou blow
>   The small rain down can rain ?
> Christ, if my love were in my arms
>   And I in my bed again !

seems to become intensified as the century wears on. But certain characteristics of this nature poetry are worth noting. In general—and there are many exceptions—the century is not interested in 'minute particulars', but in the general laws under which a series of phenomena can be brought. 'The business of the poet is not to number the streaks of the tulip' but to search for and to state broad underlying principles of poetry as of life. Out of this desire there comes the characteristic eighteenth-century poetic diction, which describes natural objects by their general characters, and establishes a particular technique to do this. The term 'grove' will stand for many different kinds of woods ; the particular is of less significance than the general. But if you read a good anthology of the age (such as Grigson's *Before the Romantics*) you will be struck, I think, with the vigour and strength of their best work : the strong momentum of the rhythm : the curious finality that comes when each line is filed and adjusted to a complete knowledge of its function. If you want to see just how well it can be done, go again to a poem that most of you will not have read since your schooldays, Gray's *Elegy in a Country Churchyard*. Its idiom has passed into our language, and familiarity has dulled its brilliance ; though not many poems have stood, as it has twice stood, the test of being repeated by men as they go into battle. But go to it, if you can, with fresh minds : read three or four stanzas aloud : and see how consummately this man contrived, with the most absolute precision, exactly what he wants to say.

> The boast of heraldry, the pomp of pow'r,
>   And all that beauty, all that wealth e'er gave,
> Awaits alike th' inevitable hour :
>   The paths of glory lead but to the grave.
>
> Nor you, ye Proud, impute to these the fault,
>   If Memory o'er their Tomb no Trophies raise,
> Where through the long-drawn aisle and fretted vault,
>   The pealing anthem swells the note of praise.

(Look in the next church you visit at the epitaphs, the coats of arms and hatchments, at the catalogues of virtues : and what they stand for.)

> Can storied urn or animated bust
> Back to its mansion call the fleeting breath ?
> Can Honour's voice provoke the silent dust,
> Or Flatt'ry soothe the dull cold ear of death ?

This eighteenth-century poetry is a strange tissue of many emotions, emotions that are, in general, kept under rigid control. It can be bitter, fantastic, scandalous, platitudinous ; it can convey the placid rivers and meadows of the Fens, or the arid heaths of East Anglia, or exploit the awe and solemnity which one felt when (as in the Roman Campagna) the ruins of dead cities and their works covered a living countryside. But if you go to it with fresh minds, you will be astonished at the strength and solidity of it ; the peace and sense of stability which it will convey : and that most satisfying finality of the thing superbly said, and by people who had a solid core of beliefs for which they had struggled.

3

To attempt to explain what we call the Romantic Movement is the most difficult task of all ; many books have been written about it, and many more will be. All we can do is to attempt to isolate some of its complicated strands.

First, I suppose, comes the general humanitarian movement, sharpened in its urgency by the horrors of the results of the Industrial Revolution in England, child-labour in the factories, the Napoleonic wars, the atrocities of the slave trade. In itself it is one part of the swing away from an intellectual and mechanical view of society, an emphasis on the heart rather than the head, the emotions rather than the intelligence. Much of the force of the movement can be traced back to the self-analysis of Rousseau, and the iconoclasm of Voltaire. As a consequence we have a new interest in unspoiled man, man uncorrupted by human institutions, by the greed and tyranny of priests and kings. The child, as unspoilt ' natural man ' (no longer a creature full of original sin which must be driven out by chastisement) becomes important in the poetry of Wordsworth and Blake ; and indeed the treatment of children in literature is an illuminating index to our changing philosophies. In the same way, peasant life, whether in Crabbe's Aldeburgh or Wordsworth's Westmorland, may hold the secret of contentment and of the noble life ; as the savage (from a convenient distance) appeared to the social philosophers to be a theoretical exponent of a ' pure ' society. You will find the idea recurring all through the nineteenth century, sometimes in a confused form, but with an heredity which can be traced backwards to the eighteenth century, through Byron's Eastern tales. At opposite poles the Sheikh literature of our time, Western films, and the advocacy by D. H. Lawrence of ' natural man ' whether as a Mexican, an Italian soldier, or a gamekeeper, are symptomatic of the same desire to return to stronger and simplified emotions.

Lightly connected with this is the strand of antiquarianism, which itself splits into two. There is a feeling abroad that the past had some secret which the present does not possess : a simpler and nobler way of living, a ' romantic ' England seen through rose-coloured spectacles. That way of thinking is by no means dead now ; it was very much alive in the later nineteenth century, when William Morris was led on from his doctrine of the joy of work, in all manner of handicrafts, to his own form of Socialism. The Restoration had in some measure shut its eyes to the past. Now it seemed that the past was a heritage of importance ; that a sense of continuity with the past was important for a sense of stability (as in the philosophy of Burke). And in addition to this the past has a capacity to produce a peculiar emotional excitement, by its strangeness, by its capacity for evoking the emotion of wonder, by the fact that it is closely linked, in many ways, to the supernatural. So what was originally a literary fashion, a carefully cultivated taste for the ' Gothick ' romantic castles, armour, ruins and the like, becomes a living reality, a sense of the world as a perpetual excitement, something strange, wonderful, with boundaries perpetually shifting and receding.

It was a supernatural world, and this was one of the most important qualities to be perceived and cultivated in the Romantic world. The ghosts and fairies of the eighteenth century are, with a very few exceptions, decorative and decorated, depicted from the teeth outward. They are creatures of ' fancy ', without any deeper roots in the human mind. Now for the first time they become alive again ; going through a strange period of growth in the Novel of Terror, nicely calculated to excite the sensibilities of the female reader (you can see that parodied in Jane Austen's *Northanger Abbey*). They grow in vitality through Scott, Melrose Abbey by moonlight and the opening of the wizard's tomb ; till the summit of achievement is that incredible world of *The Ancient Mariner*, which lives because—among other reasons—every movement of it corresponds to strange unconscious things in the depths of our minds.

The supernatural is but one aspect of the emotions of awe and wonder of the Romantic writer before a universe which had lost its certain and narrow boundaries ; in which man's spirit and his apprehensions again seemed without limits. With it came in a new wave of Hellenism which is unspent through the nineteenth century :

> I ponder how from Attic seed
> There grew an English tree,
> How Byron like his heroes fell,
> Fighting a country free,
> And Swinburne took from Shelley's lips
> The kiss of Poetry.[1]

[1] J. E. Flecker, *Oak and Olive*

With the Greek spirit there is a new emphasis on the delighted senses in all things, but particularly in the countryside. There were many reasons why it should be so ; the growing emphasis on the countryside in contrast with the smoky horror of the towns ; the sense of awe before the magnificence of mountain scenery, and a sense of pleasurable melancholy when confronted with its deserted landscapes and its ruins : the ruins which the landscape painters had brought from the Roman Campagna to

> Throw Italian light on English walls

and which the genius of the painter Richard Wilson had re-created in the English scene. Above all, perhaps, the small and individual things become important, the daffodils dancing by a lakeside, the robin redbreast in a cage as a symbol of human cruelty, the grain of sand that was a microcosm of the world. For nature is no longer to be reduced to the *genera* of things, or to the formulæ of convention, and the writers become aware of the smallest life about them, as important to their intuitive comprehension of the universe. For an example of this excited and joyful discovery of the world we may remember Coleridge's water-snakes beside the becalmed and thirst-wracked ship : a description that might be thought to embody for us much that is purest in Romantic poetry.[1]

4

But you must not think of the Romantic period as merely concerned with the cultivation of sensibility. Four great thinkers—Bentham, Malthus, Ricardo, and J. S. Mill afford the most striking contrast to the thought of the Romantic poets ; and the roots of much of our political and moral philosophy to-day can be traced backwards to their work. For the first three men attempt to strip language of emotion, and, as radical

[1] See p. 94, *ante.*

philosophers, seem to carry the methods of mathematics and science into their statements of social and economic theory. We call them, loosely, the Utilitarian School. 'Pleasure', and therefore 'value' (since the guiding principle of social science is 'the greatest happiness of the greatest number') is thought to be capable of being computed scientifically. Economics are perceived in terms of supply and demand, and of enlightened self-interest expressed in competition. If they are left to themselves, consumption and production will arrive at a state of balance through the operation of their proper laws. It is of some interest to us to-day to watch, amongst ourselves, the same philosophical confusion between 'happiness' and 'pleasure', and to consider what these philosophers would have made of the present age. But it is fair to say that most of the enlightened legislation in the twenty years that follow Waterloo is due to their influence.

Just as the mid-eighteenth century seems to us to be dominated by the literary personality of Dr. Johnson, so the first quarter or so of the nineteenth century is the age of the great and powerful literary reviews : grouped in political opposition to each other, but, on the whole, united in their suspicion and disapproval of the Romantic poets.

('Who killed John Keats?'
'I,' said *The Quarterly*.)

The *Edinburgh Review* was Whig, and both *The London Magazine* and *The Westminster Review* were radical ; *The Quarterly* and *Blackwood's* were reactionary. They drew to their staffs the most brilliant men of the time, and they laid down the law in literary matters with a bitter authoritarianism that sounds strange to-day. The Editor of *Blackwood's* killed the Editor of *The London Magazine* in a duel. Read Byron's *English Bards and Scotch Reviewers*, and see to what lengths vituperation can go. After that, read *A Vision of Judgment*.

For a commentary of another kind I recommend to you

particularly one radical writer, Cobbett of *Rural Rides* ; who will give you an unsurpassed picture of the English countryside, the rise of the new-rich landlords, the decay of agriculture, the spreading sores of the industrial towns, and particularly of London which he called ' The Wen '. And a lesser known work of his, *Advice to Young Men and Women*, is a good and wise book. To balance the picture, read another critic and satirist of Romanticism, and of the new popular education, and ' the March of Mind ', Peacock. Start with *Crotchet Castle*.

<h1 style="text-align:center">5</h1>

Of the Victorian Age it is difficult to speak ; I do not think we understand it yet, and all simplifications of it are bound to be false. But it is important that we should make the attempt : partly because our own roots are deep in that soil (however much we may deny them by a facile destructive criticism) and partly because the conflicts of our present ideologies have set up such violent emotional prejudices about it. All I can do now is to put before you certain propositions.

In the first instance it is clear to me that the ' Victorian ' age is not one age, but three, perhaps four, movements in thought and culture, with boundaries overlapping, blending into each other. The first twenty years is in part compounded of certain aftermaths of the Romantic movement. Its good sides are a steadily increasing and more widely disseminated humanitarianism in literature, a broader interest in the lives of others. The three great themes of love, death, and war are treated with an emotion which can and does become sentimental, because so much of the work is a weakened and diluted inspiration from a greater age. The last theme, war, is seen from a distance, and falsified, because there is in the national life no urgency, no pressure from without. If we are to choose two representative poems of this period for death and love, I suppose we should take both from Tennyson : *In Memoriam,* and *The Princess.*

It is, paradoxically, an age of Reason and dilute Romance, scarcely in conflict because there is, as yet, no force to bring the critical masses together. Bentham's utilitarianism and the *laissez-faire* economics of the Manchester School are one side of the materialistic picture : the other was Darwinism, and the first historical criticism of the Bible. All these combined to suggest, by an oblique and complicated process of reasoning, that Christian values had been shaken or annihilated : much as popular and half-comprehended Marxism seems to appeal to-day. About the middle of the century there is an attempt to recover the lost values, or to establish others for them : and that is why the work of the great moralists, Carlyle, Ruskin, Arnold, and Newman, seems to underline the whole thought of the age.

For it looked as if that emotional prophecy of Shelley in the *Defence* was likely to be fulfilled. Prosperity and poverty were increasing at an unparalleled rate, and a poet might have been justified in thinking that the lack of ' imagination '—by which Shelley meant, perhaps, a blend of what St. Paul called Charity and the power to develop a full sympathy with one's fellow-creatures—". . . was in a fair way to exasperate at once the extremes of luxury and want. . . . The rich have become richer, and the poor have become poorer ; and the vessel of state is driven between the Scylla and Charybdis of despotism and anarchy."

It was a kind of spiritual bankruptcy, a disruption of spiritual and moral and aesthetic values, which the moralists attacked in terms which do not differ greatly from those used by moralists in this post-war period. The remedies proposed were (as always at times when the complexity of the world seems to grow too great for the intelligence) to be found in dogma, or in some formula of simplification, or in that last resort of the idealist, a change of heart.

From our point of view the most important is the aesthetic simplification : a projection of the Keatsian formula, " Beauty is Truth, Truth Beauty." It is essential to understand how it runs through the century : from Keats to the early Tennyson, through the pre-Raphaelite poets and painters, Rossetti and Morris (with Swinburne as a kind of mechanical record-player of superb poetic skill) to the Aesthetes and the Decadents at the end of the century. At its greatest it affirms the supreme value of art : at its worst it insists on the supreme value of the artist, and his right to live in a world of his own remote from human values. The nobility of Pater leads logically to the Yellow Books, and those strange bulbous women of Aubrey Beardsley, and the long-haired poet aesthete who lunches off a lily in a glass of water, and whom you will see parodied in Gilbert and Sullivan's *Patience*. And behind them, seen as it were through a half-transparent screen, there are the brilliant social comedies of Oscar Wilde, and his personal tragedy.

I suppose that Carlyle's morality is a simplification too : a sublimated and romantic statement of the dignity of labour, a complex of all things Teutonic, and a strange violent hero-worship of great men, together with a perception of a benevolent pattern in the interpretation of history. Ruskin's was an insistence on the moral values of the aesthetic components of living : whether in painting, architecture, or social relationships, he demands above all things fidelity to what he called ' nature ', and the craftsman's labour, and the essential truth of the Gothic architecture. (We are apt to damn him for this last, seeing the new Gothic buildings that our grandfathers left us : but before we do so it is well to read his works with care, and to ponder on the mechanics of Victorian building science.) And all these simplifications had one common factor : their ' backward-gazing medievalism '. You will find it in pre-Raphaelite paintings, in Carlyle and Ruskin's eulogies of the Middle Ages and their glorification of the craftsman as against the factory mechanic : in Tennyson's rewriting of the *Morte D'Arthur* to fashion (as it might be in terms of Spenser's Twelve Moral Virtues) the Victorian landed gentry into gentlemen. And with it there went the restoration of woman to her so-called medieval pedestal of honour and ' worship ' ; perhaps as a protest, conscious or unconscious, against the growing emancipation of women (you will see these problems reflected vividly in the plays of Ibsen and Shaw) and partly because of a growing protest against the two moralities that governed the sexes. But here again we are faced with complex issues ; for the worship of woman goes back to Rossetti's strange blend of sensuality and mysticism, of soul and body united in the ecstasy of love, and forward through Coventry Patmore's *The Angel in the House.*

The medieval simplification is seen at its clearest in the writings of William Morris. He dreamed of, and practised with an astounding energy, his own peculiar kind of Socialism, in which the work of the craftsman was to be a fine and happy thing, producing all kinds of beautiful objects to equip men in their living. It was in some measure a return to the Guild system of the Middle Ages ; men were to ' forget six counties overhung with smoke, and the misery of factory labour, and the ugliness of mass-produced things '. Life in Victorian England was to become simple, and happy, among the cool water-colours of the Thames, the red brick of old houses, the brilliant colours of tapestries. And to his working and thinking he brought something of the strength and ferocity and energy of the Norse Sagas ; though he alone of all the writers knew and could present the sheer brutality as well as the colours of the Middle Ages. It is worth your while to ponder this whole question of medievalism, its truth and its falsehood : from the suburban houses of Stockbroker's Tudor to the commercialised legend of Merrie England. In your own lifetime you have heard the clangour of the conflict between G. G. Coulton and the romantic pseudo-medievalists Chesterton and Belloc. Morris' tide set in from the North and North-East : in the last twenty years of the century another current sets from the Westward, in the so-called Celtic movement. In some respects it resembles the Ossianic impulse in the middle of the eighteenth century. It died in a grey and mournful twilight because its mythology was that of scholars and not of the people : but it helped to produce in the next century, the Anglo-Irish revival and a new dramatic tradition.

The last, and from our point of view, the most complex of the simplifications is that of Matthew Arnold : in whose work the two functions of literary critic, and of the protagonist of ' culture ', meet and blend. Looking back over the first half of the century, it seemed to him that the Romantics had failed, in spite of all their sporadic individual greatness. Their work was unshaped, incomplete ; and in any event they were bad models for young poets to follow. In literature his solution was a return to the classical virtues and values, to the ages when poetry was closely linked to religion or philosophy—Aeschylus, Dante, Shakespeare, Milton—and to the great subjects of the past which remain of permanent interest because they are concerned with ultimate values. Out of his writing there comes a high cold stoicism of courage in defeat. He had found

> this strange disease of modern life
> With its sick hurry, its divided aims

and found it (as all the Victorian moralists did) profoundly disquieting. The enemies were the Philistines, the great mass of prosperous obtuse well-to-do people, whose values had become largely material, and who had grown up into wealth and power with no corresponding sense of tradition.

But his view of the very function of poetry is of central importance ; and from him, and from Coleridge, most of our modern criticism takes its source. Poetry, and the virtues that it bred, was, in some sense, destined to take the place of religion. " The strongest part of our religion to-day is its unconscious poetry." Looking back, it seemed as if the rock of Darwinism had split orthodox religion into two streams, the High Church and the Low, even into Romanism and Nonconformity : and as an example of that conflict Newman's *Apologia* remains one of the great documents of the age. (His *Idea of a University* contains more sense than many modern writings on the same subject, and has much relevance to your problem and mine.) In the eddy behind the rock were those who could not or would not accept a dogmatic solution, who could not be content to remain among the ' light half-believers of our casual creeds '. For them, poetry was of supreme importance : as a criticism of life, linked perpetually to values that had been tested by time. And because, if poetry were ' called to these high destinies ', only the best poetry would do, the critic, through whom that best was to be discovered, became of supreme importance.

I have ended here with Arnold, because, with Tennyson, he is as representative a Victorian as you will find. There are other men whose work you will use to take bearings for your point of departure : Samuel Butler of *The Way of All Flesh* (but read *Alps and Sanctuaries* too) ; Trollope and Disraeli and George Eliot ; and, for the bewilderment of a scientist before the new interpretation of Genesis, Edmund Gosse's *Father and Son*. (In that you will read how an eminent geologist and a Plymouth Brother were driven to the inexorable conclusion that God had created the fossils, as it were, ready-made.) There are hundreds more ; but as you read Butler or Gosse, Hardy or Meredith, remember always that the record of an age in its literature tends to reflect the abnormal, the unhappy, the distorted, and that happiness and contentment have little to record. It is easy to paint a grim picture of the lives of our grandfathers : it is easy—up to a point—to accept the diabolically clever picture of Lytton Strachey ; but remember that for every Victorian household as unhappy as that depicted in *The Way of All Flesh* there were—how many ?—that lived happily, and did their massive work.

I end this lecture by a quotation from a living writer, which seems pertinent to the end of this outline, and for this audience ; though it was written in 1925,[1] its accuracy of prophecy may be thought to lend weight to its authority.

It is possible, to take a single instance, that when broadcasting has ceased to be a toy, it might be the means of bringing the poet's living voice once more, as in the childhood of poetry, direct to the ears of men. It is possible that another social upheaval might liberate a new flood of hopes and energies like the French Revolution, or another war bring a new Dark Age and eventually the beginning of the whole long cycle over again. Or a new basis of society might transform men's literature together with their lives. Most Utopias indeed might well be the end of poetry, if they ever came to be established ; only, if they ever came to be established, one trusts that human nature would even more speedily be the end of Utopias. Anatole France has pictured a future world where with the human passions poetry itself has passed away and only music remains. It is not altogether a new idea ; the old-fashioned Heaven was much the same. But in fact, though the founders of cloud-cities almost always forget it, they can never really barricade their shadowy streets against the eternal forces of human unhappiness, love and jealousy and grief and separation, all the sorrows to which man delivered himself and his posterity, when he ceased to live like the beasts that are glad or grieve for the moment only, and laid bare his soul to the past that torments him and the future that dismays. Humanity could only be made perfectly happy by being so changed as to be no longer human, a new race of beings. And towards man's destiny of pain there remain two attitudes which can give at least some consolation, the best that there is to be had—the religious and the poetic. Some take one, some the other, some both. But while men have eyes for transient beauty, while they suffer and pity suffering, while they fear, and cherish courage, while they love and lose and remember, we may believe that the last poet will not find his grave.

---

[1] F. L. Lucas, *Authors Dead and Living.*

CHAPTER XI

Conclusion

AMONG the admirable American expressions which enter our language from time to time to lend it new vitality, there is one which I would have every audience, and every lecturer, use at the end of every lecture or course : *So what ?* What does all this amount to ?

Most lectures in arts subjects are futile unless they are followed up by reading on your part. All that anyone can hope to do at this stage is to suggest books of a type and range that may be new to you ; to give outline maps of this new country ; and, perhaps, to infect you with a new excitement to carry you forward into the initial stages of your exploration. I can do no more now than leave with you a series of propositions.

I

Read, in this first phase of exploration, what pleases you ; and if it pleases you, let it live with you, in your memory, and grow there. (Remember that nearly everyone has a ' good ' memory : there are few ' bad ', only ' lazy ' ones.) But most of us read far too much ephemeral literature, and we have learnt, in self defence, to forget. You may have to accustom yourself to the idea that great literature must be retained, become a part of you, live with you. You will find that it has this strange capacity to grow within you as a living organism.

Distrust all who tell you that you *ought* to like so-and-so, such-and-such, in modern poetry or art, until you have, in the first place, examined their credentials as critics, and weighed the judgments of their predecessors in critical history. Your own integrity is of infinite importance, particularly at this stage of civilization. You dare not accept opinions on literature on authority alone, any more than you would accept such opinions on politics or art. But if you start on, say, a classic whom the consensus of opinions of wise men for generations has held to be valuable, and you find that you are not in sympathy with him, it is best to lay him aside for a few months or years, and then return to him when the wall of your reading has been raised a few more courses. Then try him again. If he is still a blind spot for you, don't worry. Everyone has such. The chances are that it will all fit in, ' make sense ' as your reading builds up.

Distrust all those who tell you that there are only three novelists, or six poets, who matter, or who are ' significant ', or who show a proper ' awareness of contemporary values '. Remember that there is no easier way for the literary critic (or any other ' critic ' for that matter) to establish his own position of superiority than by deriding accepted or traditional values, or proposing an eclectic limitation of ' approved ' creative work. There have been some curious oscillations of critical opinion in the past. Do not be deluded into thinking that if modern literature or art appears to concentrate on the sordid, miserable, or frustrating elements in life it is *therefore* good or ' significant '. The destructive element is everywhere about us ; it grows in proportion as we attach an inflated value to it. Much great art is concerned with the tragedy of life, and it is partly true to say that ' our sweetest songs are those which tell of saddest thought.' : but that is because tragedy, by its nature, invites the consideration of ultimate values, and the end of the greatest tragedies is a curious and profound joy. I quote again from Yeats : " A poet creates tragedy from his soul, that soul which is alike in all men. It has not joy, as we understand that word, but ecstasy, which is from the contemplation of things vaster than the individual, and imperfectly seen, perhaps, by all those that still live." [1]

Hold closely to the doctrine of diversity of excellencies, as to that of the diversity of gifts. Build up your taste by selection from below, not by using someone else's standards imposed from above. It is very possible that, in your present stage of exploration, your ear and sense of rhythm will not take in many of the subtleties that you will afterwards perceive. You may well prefer strong and definite rhythms and you will be impatient of looser or more complex techniques. Do not worry about this ; follow your natural process of development.

Remember, if you venture into aesthetics, that you will be in a very dark forest ; and that there is not one question to be considered, but sixteen,[2] when you use the word ' beauty '. Your own answer will be a complex formula, with many variables : and these variables account for the instabilities of aesthetic judgments. In many instances deviations and inconsistencies are caused by ' impurities ', irrelevant personal or social or historical considerations, which, for various reasons, have intruded. Your test for this is most clearly apparent by comparison with another art, the architecture which you see about you every day.

Use the word ' sincerity ' with caution. You will often hear it used as if it were a test for the goodness of art of any kind. To many, I think, it denotes a kind of single-mindedness on the part of the artist, a complete identification of his own beliefs and values with those expressed in the work. This in turn suggests a *fixity* of those beliefs, which we seek to accept without question ; we call it sincerity.

Such a method of judgment seems to me to leave out of consideration the dramatic quality of much poetry. For example, the lyric is the record of a mood, and moods are, by their very

[1] *Dramatis Personæ.*
[2] See, for example, Richards, Ogden, and Wood, *The Foundations of Aesthetics.*

nature, temporary. Was it Emerson who said, " I am always insincere, as always knowing there are other moods ? " The artist is, by definition, a man of great sensibility, with a very wide range of experience. He records his moods, creates characters to express the different facets of himself. These characters speak with different voices, and become ' full ' and ' round ' in proportion as the artist possesses the power of building outwards, of synthesizing his observation of life with these projections. In this process the contradictions that appear are to be considered *either* as different aspects of the same personality, *or* as examples of the operation of the paradox, the conflict of opposites which have a resultant outside themselves.

2

I am certain that all great art is ultimately moral, as having a positive and constructive relationship to the sum of our attitudes towards life.

I am clear both from first- and second-hand experience that its value is best tested under conditions of stress in practical life.

I believe that the term *morality* includes, but is not limited by, the Ten Commandments, or perhaps what C. S. Lewis calls the *Tao* : [1] that body of collective moral values to which all men of our tradition and culture can subscribe.

The operation of the morality of art seems to me to lie on three planes. First, there is the process of sensitizing the human mind to the living world and its complexities : a sensitizing which extends in its working outwards from the experience called aesthetic into all forms of human activity.

(This is, I think, what Shelley meant in an obscure and difficult saying, ' Poetry administers to the *effect* by acting upon the *cause* ' : that is, by stimulating and sensitizing the imagination,

---

[1] *The Abolition of Man.*

it is in itself a moral agent : since the atrophy of the imagination may be, and often is, one of the causes of evil.)

In the second place, art works by confronting the mind with a scale that enables the individual to relate himself to the world in which he must live ; and, as secondary products of that knowledge, he becomes conscious of a set of experiences which he can only dimly apprehend, together with an impulse to establish a relationship with the creative forces or patterns that are presented to his consciousness thereby.

Thirdly, I believe that there is a direct moral effect through all great art, even though we are largely unconscious of its operation : for all memorable things are absorbed by us, whether music, or speech, or things seen, and recombine with the fermenting elements in ourselves that will mature in due course to form personality.

As for the imagination, I am inclined to think that Shelley was right in speaking of it as the great synthesizing and creative force in life. In the war I was struck especially by two things : how many officers of the regular army had an enthusiastic and extensive knowledge, and often the practice, of some art, and that, in general, such men were the best soldiers ; and how the great leaders seemed to possess a curious faculty of seeing into the heart of events, their significance in the present and the future, which an earlier age might have called prophecy, and which we (derisively, as was fitting) called ' crystal-gazing '. But clearly it was there. I attribute it to the phenomenon of outstandingly good brains operating at much higher speeds than the normal upon a given set of circumstances, and also to a sudden perception of what I can only describe as the rhythm of history as emerging out of time, and solidifying, as it were, in obedience to the knowledge that some seemed to possess of its inmost nature. In serving such men we became conscious that in some strange way, they were in command of events : because they knew the essence of them. Knowing that essence, they seemed able to determine, I do not know how, the pattern of things : whereas most of us evade decisions, or conform to existing circumstances, or (worst of all) are forced to improvise hastily in the wake of events.

3

Never delude yourself into thinking that you are too over-worked by your ' professional ' subject to have time for reading. There is ample time if you will only use it. It is possible, however, that the real excitement of exploration will not start till after you have left the university. Most under-graduates experience a kind of secondary delayed growth in this respect.

The process of your reading will be cumulative, but your understanding of it will increase with a sudden rapidity which I cannot explain. There seems to be a point in time—with English students it often seems to come after about eighteen to twenty months' work—when the whole pattern starts to fit together, to make sense : and men say to me : " If only I had another two years I should begin to know something about literature." That, of course, is an illusion ; but the pieces do start to come together, suddenly, in the magnetic field. One poem, one usage of language, *certifieth* another. Words are living things : full of references, overtones, shades of meaning, drawn from every context in which they have been used. Every past usage that you know is liable to bring an enrichment, a decoration, an amplification of meaning to what you read. You cannot know them all.

I do not think that there is anything which you, as scientists, need to modify in your mental processes when you are approach-ing literature. You bring to it your own great and important virtues, which are often denied to the arts student : logical habits of thought, a refusal to accept without demonstration, a general precision of approach. Many of the best students of

English I have known, and at least three of our eminent critics, were trained as mathematicians or scientists. There are, I believe, only two additional requirements. First, you must have a sense of what I can only call excited curiosity as regards the workings of the human mind in all its manifestations, and a preoccupation with the perception of the relationships—other than those which we call quantitative—of one thing to another.

The second thing you will require—and I say this with the utmost diffidence—is humility and reverence. I do not think any of us can get very far without those virtues. For in the last resort you will be faced with experiences which you can never analyse. You will have to use words as indeterminate as *Love*, or *God* : you will deal with things ' felt in the blood and felt along the heart ' : you will have to accept the extensions of meaning—the complexities if you like—which are inevitable when language is used metaphorically. If you jib at this last statement, remember that it is comparatively rarely that *any* of us use language without some admixture of its metaphorical content. Only in mathematics can you approach complete purity of diction, of universally accepted meaning conveyed by symbol. Whenever we think of causes, relationships, comparisons of value, and mental phenomena, we deal in metaphors. We cannot avoid them. It is probable (and again I say this with all humility) that the task of scientific writers of the future may well include the creation of new metaphors, new ways of explaining relationships, instead of attempting to strip language of metaphor. You have ready to your hand such a stripped language, the internationally accepted symbols of mathematics, itself beautiful and efficient. The same is partly true of the other sciences : more so, I imagine, for the physicist and the crystallo-grapher than for the botanist and zoologist. But if you listen to the following passage, you will, I think, realize that a far greater number of words carry ' images ' than most of us realize. I will try to stress such words as I read.

Suppose that the pile were to be *started* by simultaneous *release* (in the uranium metal) of N high-energy neutrons. Most of these neutrons originally have energies above the *threshold* energy of fission of U-238. However, as the neutrons pass *back and forth* in the metal and moderator, they *suffer* numerous inelastic *collisions* with the uranium and numerous elastic *collisions* with the moderator, and all these collisions *serve* to *reduce* the energies below that *threshold*. Specifically, in a typical graphite-moderated pile a neutron that has *escaped* from the uranium into the graphite *travels* on the average about 2.5 cm. between collisions and makes on the average about 200 elastic collisions before passing from the graphite back into the uranium.[1]

In the original the word *average* is also italicized, presumably to carry emphasis.

Now I have quoted this extract merely to suggest that the common idea of scientific writing as something essentially bald, direct, and unconcerned with shades of meaning or with images which carry overtones of varying degrees of complexity, is just not true. The scientific writer is often required to go far beyond the mere expression of fact. There are times when he must enlighten, persuade, convince. And there is no rule or formula for superadding ' graces ' to your writing. Never try to be ' literary '. The qualities of good writing, clarity of thought, the justness of words, the judgment implicit in imagery, must come from you, and from you alone ; and the only way of incorporating them in your own writing is by the enlargement of your sensibility, by your experience of literature of every kind, and (above all) by practice. Some index as to the confusion that so often exists is afforded by the advertisements in current journals by ' professional ' revisers who offer, for an appropriate fee, to rewrite scientific papers in a ' convincing ' manner. Again I quote from a recent statement[2] by the Cavendish professor here :

[1] *Atomic Energy*, 1945, 8–9, p. 79.
[2] At a discussion of the Report on the Regulations for the Natural Sciences Tripos. 18 October 1949.

I will try to define what I believe to be lacking in our present courses for science undergraduates. They do not learn to write clearly and briefly, marshalling their points in due and aesthetically satisfying order, and eliminating inessentials. They are inept at those turns of phrase or happy analogy which throw a flying bridge across a chasm of misunderstanding and make contact between mind and mind. They do not know how to talk to people who have had a very different training from them, and how to carry conviction when decisions on plans for action of vital importance to them are made. Those are arts which our humanists have studied, and I feel very strongly indeed that a Cambridge education for our scientists should include some contact with the humanistic side. The gift of expression is important to them as scientists ; the best research is wasted when it is extremely difficult to discover what it is all about. My experience in reading some of the papers submitted to me for publication by learned bodies makes me speak feelingly on that point. It is even more important when scientists are called upon to play their part in the world of affairs, as is happening to an increasing extent.

4

And the end of all this for you and me ? It is certain that we require what poetry has to give us : and when we understand exactly what it is that it has to give us, poetry will be dead. Your lives and mine are governed by a mixture of thought and emotion. It is possible that much of the *accidie*, of the weariness and sense of futility, in our post-war world, is to be ascribed to our failure to harness those driving forces to our policies. Disillusion and frustration are so much easier to cultivate than the positive emotions. I doubt whether anything constructive has emerged, or is likely to emerge, from a nation that believes itself to be in a state of decay. It seems to me likely that our failure is in some way due to the concentration on literature for its own sake, by men and women whose interest is in literature only. A good deal of the greatest work in the past has been done by writers to whom poetry was one activity among many. Some of you have been frightened away from poetry or art by the aesthetes who multiply in any community such as this. But they are really hollow and rather pathetic beings, people who are uncertain of themselves, and who are building up their own sense of security by a great show of sensibility and knowledge. You have no need to reckon with them.

Before all things it is needful that you should enjoy literature, as you should enjoy any skill of your mind or senses. I quote in conclusion a passage in which ' Q ' took great delight : and I can pay no greater compliment to this audience than to say with certainty how much ' Q ' would have enjoyed speaking to it.

> You never enjoy the world aright, till the Sea itself floweth in your veins, till you are clothed with the heavens, and crowned with the stars : and perceive yourself to be the sole heir of the whole world, and more than so, because men are in it who are every one sole heirs as well as you. Till you can sing and rejoice and delight in God, as misers do in gold, and Kings in sceptres, you never enjoy the world.
>
> Till your spirit filleth the whole world, and the stars are your jewels ; till you are as familiar with the ways of God in all Ages as with your walk and table : till you are intimately acquainted with that shady nothing out of which the world was made : till you love men so as to desire their happiness, with a thirst equal to the zeal of your own : till you delight in God for being good to all : you never enjoy the world. Till you more feel it than your private estate, and are more present in the hemisphere, considering the glories and the beauties there, than in your own house : Till you remember how lately you were made, and how wonderful it was when you came into it : and more rejoice in the palace of your glory, than if it had been made but to-day morning.[1]

And because it is good to see how the centuries are bridged by the thought of great men, my last quotation to follow Traherne's is from Whitehead, the mathematician and philosopher. He

[1] Traherne, *Centuries of Meditations.*

too is writing of the perception of the final harmony of things, and the secret of the union of Zest with Peace. He goes further than Traherne, for he is speaking of suffering as well as joy.

The Peace that is here meant is not the negative conception of anæsthesia. It is a positive feeling which crowns the 'life and motion' of the soul. It is hard to define, and difficult to speak of. It is not a hope for the future, nor is it an interest in present details. It is a broadening of feeling due to the emergence of some deep metaphysical insight, unverbalized and yet momentous in its co-ordination of values. Its first effect is the removal of the stress of acquisitive feeling arising from the soul's preoccupation with itself.[1]

---

[1] A. N. Whitehead, *Adventures of Ideas*, p. 367.

Poems and Passages used in the Text

CHAPTER II

(i)

The Twa Corbies

I

As I was walking all alane,
I heard twa corbies making a mane :
The tane unto the tither did say,
' Whar sall we gang and dine the day ? '

II

'—In behint yon auld fail dyke
I wot there lies a new-slain knight ;
And naebody kens that he lies there
But his hawk, his hound, and his lady fair.

III

' His hound is to the hunting gane,
His hawk to fetch the wild-fowl hame,
His lady's ta'en anither make,
So we may mak' our dinner sweet.

IV

' Ye'll sit on his white hause-bane,
And I'll pike out his bonny blue e'en :
Wi' ae lock o' his gowden hair
We'll theek our nest when it grows bare.

V

'Mony a one for him maks mane,
But nane sall ken whar he is gane :
O'er his white banes, when they are bare,
The wind sall blaw for evermair.'

ANONYMOUS

corbies] ravens.　　　　fail] turf.　　　　hause] neck.　　　　theek] thatch.

(ii)

A Valediction : forbidding mourning

As virtuous men passe mildly away,
　And whisper to their soules, to goe,
Whilst some of their sad friends doe say,
　The breath goes now, and some say, no :

So let us melt, and make no noise,
　No teare-floods, nor sigh-tempests move,
'Twere prophanation of our joyes
　To tell the layetie our love.

Moving of th'earth brings harmes and feares,
　Men reckon what it did and meant,
But trepidation of the spheres,
　Though greater farre, is innocent.

Dull sublunary lovers love
　(Whose soule is sense) cannot admit
Absence, because it doth remove
　Those things which elemented it.

But we by a love, so much refin'd,
　That our selves know not what it is,
Inter-assured of the mind,
　Care lesse, eyes, lips, and hands to misse.

Our two soules therefore, which are one,
　Though I must goe, endure not yet
A breach, but an expansion,
　Like gold to ayery thinnesse beate.

146

If they be two, they are two so
  As stiffe twin compasses are two,
Thy soule the fixt foot, makes no show
  To move, but doth, if th'other doe.

And though it in the center sit,
  Yet when the other far doth rome,
It leanes, and hearkens after it,
  And growes erect, as that comes home.

Such wilt thou be to mee, who must
  Like th'other foot, obliquely runne ;
Thy firmnes makes my circle just,
  And makes me end, where I begunne.

JOHN DONNE

CHAPTER III

(i)

To His Coy Mistress

Had we but world enough, and time,
This coyness, Lady, were no crime.
We would sit down and think which way
To walk and pass our long love's day.
Thou by the Indian Ganges' side
Shouldst rubies find : I by the tide
Of Humber would complain. I would
Love you ten years before the Flood,
And you should, if you please, refuse
Till the conversion of the Jews.
My vegetable love should grow
Vaster than empires, and more slow ;
An hundred years should go to praise
Thine eyes and on thy forehead gaze ;
Two hundred to adore each breast,
But thirty thousand to the rest ;
An age at least to every part,
And the last age should show your heart.
For, Lady, you deserve this state,
Nor would I love at lower rate.

147

But at my back I always hear
Time's wingèd chariot hurrying near ;
And yonder all before us lie
Deserts of vast eternity.
Thy beauty shall no more be found,
Nor, in thy marble vault, shall sound
My echoing song : then worms shall try
That long preserved virginity,
And your quaint honour turn to dust,
And into ashes all my lust :
The grave's a fine and private place,
But none, I think, do there embrace.
  Now therefore, while the youthful hue
Sits on thy skin like morning [dew]
And while thy willing soul transpires
At every pore with instant fires,
Now let us sport us while we may,
And now, like amorous birds of prey,
Rather at once our time devour
Than languish in his slow-chapt power.
Let us roll all our strength and all
Our sweetness up into one ball,
And tear our pleasures with rough strife
Thorough the iron gates of life :
Thus, though we cannot make our sun
Stand still, yet we will make him run.

ANDREW MARVELL

(ii)

A Slumber did my Spirit Seal

A slumber did my spirit seal ;
  I had no human fears :
She seem'd a thing that could not feel
  The touch of earthly years.

No motion has she now, no force ;
  She neither hears nor sees ;
Roll'd round in earth's diurnal course,
  With rocks, and stones, and trees.

WORDSWORTH

(i)

The Sick Rose

O Rose, thou art sick !
The invisible worm,
That flies in the night,
In the howling storm,

Has found out thy bed
Of crimson joy ;
And his dark secret love
Does thy life destroy.

WILLIAM BLAKE, *Songs of Experience*

(ii)

The Fire Sermon

The river's tent is broken : the last fingers of leaf
Clutch and sink into the wet bank. The wind
Crosses the brown land, unheard. The nymphs are departed.
Sweet Thames, run softly, till I end my song.
The river bears no empty bottles, sandwich papers,
Silk handkerchiefs, cardboard boxes, cigarette ends
Or other testimony of summer nights. The nymphs are departed.
And their friends, the loitering heirs of city directors ;
Departed, have left no addresses.
By the waters of Leman I sat down and wept . . .
Sweet Thames, run softly till I end my song,
Sweet Thames, run softly, for I speak not loud or long.
But at my back in a cold blast I hear
The rattle of the bones, and chuckle spread from ear to ear.

A rat crept softly through the vegetation
Dragging its slimy belly on the bank
While I was fishing in the dull canal
On a winter evening round behind the gashouse

Musing upon the king my brother's wreck
And on the king my father's death before him.
White bodies naked on the low damp ground
And bones cast in a little low dry garret,
Rattled by the rat's foot only, year to year.
But at my back from time to time I hear
The sound of horns and motors, which shall bring
Sweeney to Mrs. Porter in the spring.
O the moon shone bright on Mrs. Porter
And on her daughter
They wash their feet in soda water
Et O ces voix d'enfants, chantant dans la coupole !

Twit twit twit
Jug jug jug jug jug jug
So rudely forc'd.
Tereu.

Unreal City
Under the brown fog of a winter noon
Mr. Eugenides, the Smyrna merchant
Unshaven, with a pocket full of currants
C.i.f. London : documents at sight,
Asked me in demotic French
To luncheon at the Cannon Street Hotel
Followed by a weekend at the Metropole.

T. S. ELIOT

CHAPTER V

(i)

The Stare's Nest by My Window

The bees build in the crevices
Of loosening masonry, and there
The mother birds bring grubs and flies.
My wall is loosening ; honey-bees,
Come build in the empty house of the stare.

We are closed in, and the key is turned
On our uncertainty ; somewhere
A man is killed, or a house burned,
Yet no clear fact to be discerned :
Come build in the empty house of the stare.

A barricade of stone or of wood ;
Some fourteen days of civil war ;
Last night they trundled down the road
That dead young soldier in his blood :
Come build in the empty house of the stare.

We had fed the heart on fantasies,
The heart's grown brutal from the fare ;
More substance in our enmities
Than in our love ; O honey-bees,
Come build in the empty house of the stare.

W. B. YEATS

(ii)

Before the World was Made

If I make the lashes dark
And the eyes more bright
And the lips more scarlet,
Or ask if all be right
From mirror after mirror,
No vanity's displayed :
I'm looking for the face I had
Before the world was made.

What if I look upon a man
As though on my beloved,
And my blood be cold the while
And my heart unmoved ?
Why should he think me cruel
Or that he is betrayed ?
I'd have him love the thing that was
Before the world was made.

W. B. YEATS

CHAPTER VI

(i)

                 Besides, this Duncan
Hath borne his faculties so meek, hath been
So clear in his great office, that his virtues
Will plead like angels trumpet-tongu'd against
The deep damnation of his taking-off ;
And pity, like a naked new-born babe,
Striding the blast, or heaven's cherubin, hors'd
Upon the sightless couriers of the air,
Shall blow the horrid deed in every eye,
That tears shall drown the wind. I have no spur
To prick the sides of my intent, but only
Vaulting ambition, which o'erleaps itself
And falls on the other.—
      [*Enter* LADY MACBETH]
             How now ! what news ?
                Macbeth, i, 7, 16

(ii)

  No, no, no, no ! Come, let's away to prison ;
We two alone will sing like birds i' the cage :
When thou dost ask me blessing, I'll kneel down,
And ask of thee forgiveness : so we'll live,
And pray, and sing, and tell old tales, and laugh
At gilded butterflies, and hear poor rogues
Talk of court news ; and we'll talk with them too,
Who loses and who wins ; who's in, who's out ;
And take upon's the mystery of things,
As if we were God's spies : and we'll wear out,
In a wall'd prison, packs and sets of great ones
That ebb and flow by the moon.
                King Lear, v, 3, 8

(i)

And the doors shall be shut in the streets,
when the sound of the grinding is low,
and he shall rise up at the voice of the bird,
and all the daughters of music shall be brought low :
Also when they shall be afraid of that which is high,
and fears shall be in the way,
and the almond tree shall flourish,
and the grasshopper shall be a burden,
and desire shall fail :
because man goeth to his long home,
and the mourners go about the streets :
Or ever the silver cord be loosed,
or the golden bowl be broken,
or the pitcher be broken at the fountain,
or the wheel broken at the cistern.
Then shall the dust return to the earth as it was ;
and the spirit shall return unto God who gave it.

The Book of Ecclesiastes, xii, 4–7

(ii)

Lay not up for yourselves treasures upon earth, where moth and rust doth corrupt, and where thieves break through and steal :

But lay up for yourselves treasures in heaven, where neither moth nor rust doth corrupt, and where thieves do not break through nor steal :

For where your treasure is, there will your heart be also.

The light of the body is the eye : if therefore thine eye be single, thy whole body shall be full of light :

But if thine eye be evil, thy whole body shall be full of darkness. If therefore the light that is in thee be darkness, how great is that darkness !

No man can serve two masters : for either he will hate the one, and love the other ; or else he will hold to the one, and despise the other. Ye cannot serve God and mammon.

Therefore I say unto you, Take no thought for your life, what ye shall eat, or what ye shall drink ; nor yet for your body, what ye shall put on. Is not the life more than meat, and the body than raiment ?

Behold the fowls of the air : for they sow not, neither do they reap, nor gather into barns ; yet your heavenly Father feedeth them. Are ye not much better than they ?

Which of you by taking thought can add one cubit unto his stature ?

And why take ye thought for raiment ? Consider the lilies of the field, how they grow ; they toil not, neither do they spin :

And yet I say unto you, That even Solomon in all his glory was not arrayed like one of these.

Wherefore, if God so clothe the grass of the field, which today is, and tomorrow is cast into the oven, shall he not much more clothe you, O ye of little faith ?

Therefore take no thought, saying, What shall we eat ? or, What shall we drink ? or, Wherewithal shall we be clothed ?

(For after all these things do the Gentiles seek :) for your heavenly Father knoweth that ye have need of all these things.

But seek ye first the kingdom of God, and his righteousness ; and all these things shall be added unto you.

Take therefore no thought for the morrow : for the morrow shall take thought for the things of itself. Sufficient unto the day is the evil thereof.

The Gospel according to St. Matthew, vi

CHAPTER VIII

(i)

From the Epistle to Dr. Arbuthnot

Peace to all such ! but were there One whose fires
True Genius kindles, and fair Fame inspires ;
Blest with each talent and each art to please,
And born to write, converse, and live with ease :
Should such a man, too fond to rule alone,
Bear, like the Turk, no brother near the throne.
View him with scornful, yet with jealous eyes,
And hate for arts that caus'd himself to rise ;

Damn with faint praise, assent with civil leer,
And without sneering, teach the rest to sneer ;
Willing to wound, and yet afraid to strike,
Just hint a fault, and hesitate dislike ;
Alike reserv'd to blame, or to commend,
A tim'rous foe, and a suspicious friend ;
Dreading ev'n fools, by Flatterers besieg'd,
And so obliging, that he ne'er oblig'd ;
Like *Cato*, give his little Senate laws,
And sit attentive to his own applause ;
While Wits and Templars ev'ry sentence raise,
And wonder with a foolish face of praise :——
Who but must laugh, if such a man there be ?
Who would not weep, if ATTICUS were he ?

POPE

(ii)

The Scribe

What lovely things
   Thy hand hath made :
The smooth-plumed bird
   In its emerald shade,
The seed of the grass,
   The speck of stone
Which the wayfaring ant
   Stirs—and hastes on !

Though I should sit
   By some tarn in thy hills,
Using its ink
   As the spirit wills
To write of Earth's wonders,
   Its live, willed things,
Flit would the ages
   On soundless wings
Ere unto Z
   My pen drew nigh ;
Leviathan told,
   And the honey-fly :

And still would remain
  My wit to try—
My worn reeds broken,
  The dark tarn dry,
All words forgotten—
  Thou, Lord, and I.

WALTER DE LA MARE

This table, and the list of books following it, is intended for use in connection with Chapters IX and X

DANTE	1265–1321	Inferno, Paradiso	Roger Bacon 1214–1293 ? Liturgical Drama 1320
BOCCACCIO	1313–1375	Decameron	Hundred Years' War begins 1337
PETRARCH	1304–1374	Sonnets to Laura	Chester, York, Wakefield Plays 1330–1350
WYCLIF	1324?–1384	Bible	The Black Death 1348
CHAUCER	1340?–1400	Prologue, Nuns Priest Tale, Pardoner's Tale	The Great Papal Schism 1378
LANGLAND	1330?–1400	Piers Plowman	Peasants' Revolt 1381
HENRYSON	1425–1500	Testament of Cresseid, Fables	King's College Chapel begun 1446 Fall of Constantinople 1453
MALORY	?–1471	Morte d'Arthur	Gutenberg's Printing Press 1454
DUNBAR	1460?–1520?	Lament for the Makaris	Caxton's Press 1477 Columbus discovers America 1492
MORE	1478–1535	Utopia	Copernicus 1473–1543
MACHIAVELLI	1469–1527	The Prince	Leonardo da Vinci 1452–1514
JOHN KNOX	1505–1572	First Blast of the Trumpet, Pamphlets	Magellan's Voyage 1519–1521
WYATT	1503–1542	Lyrics	Dissolution of the Monasteries 1537
ASCHAM	1515–1568	Schoolmaster, Toxophilus	Many Grammar Schools founded 1550–1600
SURREY	1517–1547	Lyrics	The Great Bible placed in Churches 1539
MONTAIGNE	1533–1592	Essays	Queen Elizabeth 1558–1603
SIDNEY	1554–1586	Arcadia, Apologie, Sonnets	Drake sees the Pacific 1577 Holinshed's Chronicles 1578
SPENSER	1552–1599	Prothalamion, Epithalamion, The Faerie Queene 1, 4	Galileo 1564–1642 Mercator's Atlas 1585–1595

BACON	1561–1626	Essays, Advancement, New Atlantis	Armada 1588
MARLOWE	1564–1593	Faustus, Jew of Malta, Edward II	Kepler 1571–1630
SHAKESPEARE	1564–1616		Great Court of Trinity c. 1600
DONNE	1573–1631	Songs and Sonnets	Gilbert's de Magnete 1600
BEN JONSON	1573–1637	Alchemist, Volpone, Every Man in his Humour	Authorized Version 1611 Napier's Logarithms 1614
WEBSTER	1580–1625	White Devil, Duchess of Malfi	
MILTON	1608–1674	Minor Poems, Samson, Paradise Lost 1, 7, 8	Death of Cervantes 1616
BROWNE	1605–1682	Urn Burial, Religio Medici, Vulgar Errors	John Ray 1627–1705
WALTON	1593–1683	The Compleat Angler, Lives	Harvey's theory of the Circulatio of the Blood 1628
HERRICK	1591–1674	Hesperides	Boyle 1626–1691 Execution of Charles I 1649
HERBERT	1593–1633	Selected Poems	The Royal Society 1660
MARVELL	1621–1678	Selected Poems	Leeuwenhoek 1632–1723
DRYDEN	1631–1700	Absalom and Achitophel, Annus Mirabilis, Shorter Poems	Library of Trinity designed 167:
PEPYS	1632–1703	Diary	Christopher Wren 1632–1723
EVELYN	1620–1706	Diary	Newton 1642–1727
AUBREY	1626–1697	Brief Lives	Restoration Comedy and Tragedy
BUNYAN	1628–1688	Life and Death of Mr. Badman, Pilgrim's Progress	The Great Fire 1666
DEFOE	1660–1731	Journal of the Plague Year, Moll Flanders	Paradise Lost, 1667
SWIFT	1667–1745	Gulliver, Modest Proposal, Advice to Servants	The British Revolution 1868
ADDISON	1672–1719	Selected Essays	Richard Wilson 1714–1782
STEELE	1672–1729	Selected Essays	Senate House begun 1722
POPE	1688–1744	Rape of the Lock, Dunciad, Epistle to Arbuthnot	Linnæus' Systema Naturae 1735
RICHARDSON	1689–1761	Pamela, Clarissa Harlowe	Hogarth 1697–1764
FIELDING	1707–1754	Tom Jones, Joseph Andrews	Buffon 1707–1788
SMOLLETT	1721–1771	Peregrine Pickle, Humphry Clinker	Robert Adam 1728–1792

158

STERNE	1713–1768	Sentimental Journey, Tristram Shandy	Macpherson's Fingal 1761
JOHNSON	1709–1784	Rasselas, Life of Savage, Preface to Shakespeare	Percy's Reliques 1765
GRAY	1716–1771	Poems, Letters	Reynolds 1723–1792
GOLDSMITH	1728–1774	Deserted Village, Vicar of Wakefield	Gainsborough 1727–1788
COWPER	1731–1800	Task, Selected Letters	Aloisio Galvani 1737–1798
CRABBE	1754–1832	Village, Tales of the Hall	James Watt 1736–1819
BURKE	1729–1797	Reflections on the French Revolution	American War of Independence 1776
GIBBON	1737–1794	Autobiography, Age of the Antonines	Fall of the Bastille 1789 Jeremy Bentham 1748–1832
BLAKE	1757–1827	Poetical Sketches, Songs of Innocence	John Dalton 1776–1844 (Atomic Theory 1808)
WORDSWORTH	1770–1850	Lyrical Ballads Prelude, Bks. 1, 2, 4	Faraday 1791–1867
COLERIDGE	1772–1834	Lyric Poems, Ancient Mariner, Christabel	Malthus' Essay of Population 1798
KEATS	1795–1821	Poems 1820, Hyperion	Waterloo 1815
SHELLEY	1792–1822	Prometheus Unbound	The first Factory Act 1819
BYRON	1788–1824	Don Juan, The Vision of Judgement, Lyrics	Revolt of Greece against the Turks 1821 Adam Sedgwick 1785–1873
SCOTT	1771–1832	Lay of the last Minstrel, Kenilworth	Charles Darwin 1809–1882
JANE AUSTEN	1775–1817	Pride and Prejudice, Emma	T. H. Huxley 1825–1895
LAMB	1775–1834	Essays of Elia, Letters	Gregor Mendel 1822–1884
PEACOCK	1785–1866	Crotchet Castle, Nightmare Abbey	Constable's Leaping Horse 1825
TROLLOPE	1815–1882	Barchester Towers	Reform Act 1832
BORROW	1803–1881	Lavengro, Wild Wales	Tracts for the Times 1833–1841
DISRAELI	1804–1881	Coningsby, Sybil	The Year of Revolutions—1848
NEWMAN	1801–1890	Apologia, Idea of a University	The Great Exhibition 1851
TENNYSON	1809–1892	Poems 1842, In Memoriam, Maud	Discovery of Neanderthal Man 1856
THACKERAY	1811–1863	Vanity Fair, The Four Georges	Pre-Raphaelite Brotherhood 1848
BROWNING	1812–1889	Men and Women, Dramatis Personæ	Crimean War 1854–1856 Origin of Species 1859

C. Brontë	1816–1855	*Jane Eyre, Villette*	
E. Brontë	1818–1848	*Wuthering Heights*	
Dickens	1812–1870	*Sketches by Boz, Bleak House*	*Alice in Wonderland* 1865
G. Eliot	1819–1880	*Adam Bede, Silas Marner, Middlemarch*	
Rossetti	1828–1882	Selected Poems	U.S. Civil War 1861–1865 Franco-Prussian War 1870
Morris	1834–1896	*Defence of Guenevere, Sigurd, News from Nowhere*	Photography discovered
Arnold	1822–1888	Poems 1853	Test Act repealed 1871
Swinburne	1837–1909	*Poems and Ballads 1 and 2*	Clerk Maxwell's Electromagnetic Theory of Light 1873
Meredith	1828–1909	*Evan Harrington*	T. H. Green's *Prolegomena to Ethics* 1883
Moore	1857–1933	*The Brook Kerith, Hail and Farewell*	Gladstone's Irish Home Rule Bill 1886
Butler	1835–1902	*Erewhon, Notebooks, Alps and Sanctuaries*	Frazer's *Golden Bough* 1890
Hardy	1840–1928	*Woodlanders, Selected Poems*	First Great Trade Depression 1873–1896
Hopkins	1844–1889	*Poems*	
Conrad	1857–1924	*Lord Jim, Youth, Typhoon*	Boer War 1899
Wilde	1856–1900	*Importance of being Earnest, Ballad of Reading Gaol*	Rutherford 1871–1937
Kipling	1865–1936	*Traffics and Discoveries, Selected Poems*	Pavlov's dogs 1904–on
Housman	1859–1936	*Shropshire Lad, Last Poems*	Hopkins on Vitamins 1912
Yeats	1865–1939	*The Tower, The Winding Stair*	
Wells	1866–1946	*Kipps, Tono-Bungay*	Einstein's Relativity 1915
Bennett	1867–1931	*Old Wives' Tale, Tales of the Five Towns*	First World War 1914

A SELECTION FOR CASUAL READING

ANTHOLOGIES

The various Oxford Books : *Verse, Prose, Modern Verse, Ballads*, etc.

Logan Pearsall Smith. *A Treasury of English Prose.*
Robert Bridges. *The Spirit of Man.*
W. T. Young. *Poetry of the Age of Shakespeare.*
H. J. C. Grierson. *Metaphysical Poetry from Donne to Butler.*
Herbert Reed. *The Knapsack.*
C. H. Wilkinson. *Diversions.*

MISCELLANEOUS

R. G. Collingwood. *An Autobiography.*
Boswell. *Journal of a Tour to the Hebrides.*
Edmund Gosse. *Father and Son.*
Walter Pater. *The Renaissance.*
E. M. W. Tillyard. *The Elizabethan World Picture.*
G. M. Trevelyan. *English Social History.*
Samuel Butler. *Notebooks. The Way of All Flesh.*
Darwin. *A Naturalist's Voyage in H.M.S. Beagle.*
Lowes Dickinson. *The Greek View of Life.*
J. Summerson. *Georgian England.*
Burton. *Anatomy of Melancholy.*
A. N. Whitehead. *Adventures of Ideas.*
Sterne. *Tristram Shandy.*
S. C. Roberts. *Samuel Johnson, Writer.*
Lytton Strachey. *Eminent Victorians.*

Richard Jefferies. *The Amateur Poacher.*

Eileen Power. *Medieval People.*

G. G. Coulton. *Medieval Panorama.*

Peacock. *Crochet Castle.*

Kinglake. *Eothen.*

Virginia Woolf. *The Common Reader.*

Hesketh Pearson. *The Smith of Smiths.*

Pepys. *Diary.*

Aubrey. *Brief Lives and other Selected Writings.*

R. H. Wilenski. *English Painting.*

Montaigne. *Essays.*

Logan Pearsall Smith. *Trivia.*

G. N. Clark. *Science and Technology in the Age of Newton.*

Basil Willey *The Seventeenth Century Background*

L. Mumford. *The Culture of Cities.*

Edith Sitwell. *A Poet's Notebook.*

INDEX

Addison, 89
Aeschylus, 43, 131
à Kempis, St. Thomas, 93
Allt, G. P. D., xvi
Ariosto, 109
Aristotle, 100
Arnold, Matthew, 1, 35, 54, 128, 131, 132
Ascham, Roger, 108
Ashley, Wilfred, 11
Atomic Energy, Report of Commission on, 141
Aubrey, John, 114, 116
Austen, Jane, 124

Beardsley, Aubrey, 129
Belloc, Hilaire, 11, 87, 130
Bentham, J., 125, 128
Bible, The, xii, xv, 6, 29, 54, 69, 78, 86, 128
   Acts, 81, 84–5, 108
   Corinthians, 16 n., 81
   Ecclesiastes, 71–80
   Genesis, 132
   Job, 96
   Matthew, 81–4
   Proverbs, 96
   Psalms, 43, 45
   Revelations, 81
   Solomon, Song of, 20
Blackwood's Magazine, 126
Blake, William, 56, 62, 95, 123
   Pity, 62
   The Sick Rose, 4, 26, 39–41, 42
   Songs of Innocence, 96

Boccaccio, 105
Bodkin, Maud, 6
Boyle, 111
Bradbrook, M. C., 32 n.
Bragg, Prof. Sir W. L., vii–ix, 141
Browne, Sir Thomas, 15, 16, 93, 111, 112
Browning, 11
Bunyan, 116
Burke, 123
Burns, 2
Burton, Richard, 112
Butler, Samuel (*Erewhon*), 132
Byron, 104, 123, 126

Campbell, Roy, 87–8
Campion, 74
Carlyle, 128, 129
Chambers, R. W., 100 n.
Chambers and Sidgwick, 120 n.
Character Writers, The, 116
Chaucer, 103, 105
Chesterton, G. K., 87, 130
Cobbett, W., 127
Coleridge, 131
   The Ancient Mariner, 6, 94, 124, 125
   Kubla Khan, 9
Collier, J., 116
Collins, William, 120
Constable, 94
Constantinople, 100, 106
Coulton, G. G., 86 n., 87, 130
Coverdale, 80

163